Gweilo Moments

Gweilo Moments

*Notes from Hong Kong on Life,
Motherhood, Cats and Adoption*

Robin Minietta

Chameleon Press

GWEILO MOMENTS
© 2005 Robin Minietta
ISBN 988-97061-7-2

Published by Chameleon Press
23rd Floor, 245–251 Hennessy Road, Hong Kong
www.chameleonpress.com

Typeset in Adobe Garamond by Alan Sargent

Printed and bound in the United Kingdom and the United States
First printing March 2005
Second printing June 2005

Supported by

香 港 藝 術 發 展 局
Hong Kong Arts Development Council

The Hong Kong Arts Development Council fully supports freedom
of expression. The views and opinions expressed in this publication,
and the entire contents thereof, are those of the author and do not
represent the stand of the Council.

Contents

For my mother
Frances Stewart Minietta

Skipping rocks in Hong Kong

M Y YOUNGEST DAUGHTER, Natalie, is not quite one year old. Sera, my first-born, has just turned two. I am forty; my sister, forty-one. My mother is sixty-eight. Her mother, Nana, has been dead for fifteen years. My Aunt Pat is seventy-seven; Aunt Peg is one year younger.

Today is my birthday, and this year, the numbers are troubling me. I calculate as I run errands: my mother is twenty-eight years older than me, sixty-six years older than Sera — an easy, gracious spread between mother, daughter, and grand-daughter. When Sera turns forty, I will be seventy-eight: a less gracious calculation. When Natalie turns forty, my sister will be eighty. What to make of that?

What to make of any of this? Why am I running these numbers, carrying out this peculiar accounting? Then I realize — it's not about the numbers. What I am doing on the occasion of my fortieth birthday is tracing out relationships, mapping human coordinates, reassuring myself that my daughters and I are indeed inextricably enmeshed in the family matriarchy. I am living on Hong Kong Island, a world away from the women who have filled my life, and as I step into a new decade, I feel the full measure of the miles. I imagine walking down to the water's edge and, with a strong snap of the wrist, skipping rocks out across the South China Sea, past Taiwan, past the islands off the southern tip of Japan, past Hawaii; the rocks, powered by my need to pull the continents closer, spinning and ricocheting off the crests of the Pacific Ocean to their destination on the west coast of the United States — to my mother in Seattle, to my aunts in Los Angeles, to my sister on one of the small islands of South Puget Sound. I imagine these women bending to pick the rocks from the shoreline, brushing the sand off with their fingertips, and skimming them back to me in acknowledgement.

My family, particularly on my mother's side, does not grow many men. The females come in pairs, typically two girls to each boy, or in threesomes — as if the *y*-chromosomes simply cannot find a way to muscle into the parade of *x*s. The pattern holds across generations, across first and second cousins, across marriages and remarriages. My father, one of three boys, is the exception. But even there, two of the three sons managed to land in households dominated by women.

There are also not many nondescript women in my family. Gather a gaggle of us in one room, and listen to the stories fly — most of them true (though perhaps embellished), and nearly all of them entertaining (the duds having been weeded out on previous occasions). There is my Aunt Peg, star of Hollywood westerns and veteran of countless television dramas and commercials. When she has her narcolepsy under control, she is a wonderful raconteur. My Aunt Pat, not to be outdone, has her own back-stage stories — most famously, about her role as voice coach to Vivien Leigh. Leigh's southern accent for her role as Scarlett O'Hara in *Gone With the Wind* needed work, or so the story goes; the job fell to my aunt. My mother can also hold an audience — she recently arrived late to a family dinner, explaining that she had been involved in negotiating an end to a hostage crisis — a not so uncommon event in her work as a counselor to perpetrators of domestic violence. One of her clients had somehow managed to snatch a gun away from the policeman who had arrested him, and was holding three officers hostage inside a police station. My mother, unimpressed, told him he was a goddamned fool, and to give her the gun before he hurt himself. He did.

But for all the talent and charm of these women, this is no honey-coated Oprah-style girl-power matriarchy. And there's the rub. The demons that have hitched a ride on our strands of DNA are persistent, destructive, and wily. Alcoholism has ripped through one part of the family, nearly gutting it with breath-taking viciousness. It began, it seems, in the Deep South, with my great-grandmother, Biggie (her given name forever obscured by her girth). Biggie's drinking was a quiet problem, as befitted a wealthy daughter of the Confederacy, and one that emerged late in life, well after she had raised her family and amassed a million-dollar fortune running a hardware store and a Ford dealership. Although she spent her last decade housebound, subsisting on bourbon, ice cream, and lemon cake, alcohol did not swallow the best part of her life. The next generation was less lucky. My grandmother escaped a serious drinking problem by a thread, while her brother drowned a stellar naval career and numerous marriages in tumblers of hard liquor — a self-inflicted ruination that still has the power to make those in my family who knew him wince.

My aunt's experience with the disease has much the same effect. Long a social drinker, Pat started drinking in earnest after her husband, an actor and war hero, collapsed on the deck of a naval battleship during a change of command ceremony and died at forty-three of a heart attack. A well-stocked bar was Pat's solace and anesthesia, and for many long, brutal years she lost herself in an alcoholic miasma. That she found her way out is one of my family's most cherished triumphs.

Perhaps this particular torment flamed out doing battle with my aunt. Perhaps it is marking time. Susceptible, all of us, we stand alert, watching out for this one, taking care not to let it get a foothold in each other's lives.

While alcoholism claims center-stage as the most visible scar among us, it is not the only one. More damaging to my immediate family is my grandmother's bequest. Born and raised in Southern-style privilege, Nana spent a lifetime cloaked in self-effacing gentility. It may once have served her well; God knows what it took for a smart, creative woman to survive the narrowly conceived world that was laid out for her in Bessemer, Alabama in the early 1900s. But over the years, the guise got twisted — I suspect the act simply got away from her — and self-effacement became self-deprecation, gentility became rigidity, and Nana shrank into near-silent martyrdom, quick to take offense, quicker still to suffer. She was pained; she disapproved. She made us pay.

Relationships ruptured in the late 1970s, when my grandmother abruptly packed up and moved to Los Angeles, putting as many miles as she could manage between herself and our family home in Seattle. It was payback, punishment meted out to my mother for her attempt to come to terms with a painful childhood episode — another quicksilver departure, this one coming after the collapse of Nana's third marriage. That Nana would have felt the need to leave Atlanta and her husband, my mother could understand. That Nana would leave her behind — a six-year-old — cut so deeply that the wound has yet to fully heal. She took her two eldest daughters, but left her youngest behind. Why? What special burden did my mother represent? It seems like a fair-enough question to ask, but beyond offering up a one-size-fits-all disclaimer — "I had no choice" — my grandmother had little to say. She left town so quickly, she neglected to close out her bank accounts.

So there. That's how we were trained to settle conflict in my family. Retreat. Shut the door. Freeze out the offending party. Turn your back, withdraw into silence, act deeply aggrieved. Refuse responsibility. Take your pick: deployed with skill, they are all highly effective.

My mother and I were Nana's best pupils. Between us, we spent decades perfecting our talents, decades more trying to undo the damage — the worst of which boomeranged and nearly permanently disabled our ability to form healthy adult relationships. The details are gruesome, and we'll skip them for now. Let's leave it here: my mother, with near super-human courage, chose to go *mano-a-mano* with her past — and past-patterns — and came out the winner. I eventually followed her lead, but only because I had sunk so low that I had little choice.

So why, on the occasion of my fortieth birthday, am I reassured and comforted by my blood-ties to this matriarchy? Why do I want this birthright for my daughters? If there is anywhere in the world I could isolate myself from family archetypes and set to work on creating new ones, it is here in Hong Kong. Short of my husband, no one in this city knows me intimately enough to have any expectations about my behavior, my reaction to stress or to conflict. But I have come to realize that I do not want a fresh start, that my past mistakes provide me with an insurance policy of sorts — I know just how bad it gets going down the rutted roads I have previously chosen, and I'm not going back. Not ever. I can say that with a certainty that comes only from being branded by experience. And if I make allowances for my mistakes, surely I owe the same consideration to the women I love — women, who, on the whole, have afforded me more kindness, more affection than I have them. I have never felt harshly judged by them, even when I most deserved it. Now, after skirting the edges of the matriarchy for many years, I am learning to appreciate the women who spool out from the nucleus of my immediate family for their exuberant, no-holds-barred personalities; for their ability to charge at the world despite having been flung hard to the ground more than once; and for their deep loyalty to each other.

I pause, and I consider the inherited patterns that have shaped my life. My daughters have forced the issue. I dare not go at this blindly or unthinkingly; they deserve better. Much of the hard work has been done already — the Splanes and Stewarts, the Morrises, the Miniettas: we have given enough of our lives to rooting out the demons. Surely the next generation will be seeded with our victories.

Our matriarchy began a century and a half ago with Velma Calhoun Long, my great-great-great-grandmother, a teacher and minister, born 1855, died 1924. My daughter Natalie Stewart Wheeler, born December 15, 1998, is its most recent arrival. Their lives frame a legacy worth note.

"Hello, hello?"

I T'S LUNCHTIME, and the phone is ringing. It's Hongkong Telecom, and a voice speaks to me in heavily accented English. "Hello, ahhh, I'm calling about your new telephone number." What new telephone number? I lose the next few lines of the conversation to the accent, but pick it up again when the caller repeats a single word three or four times. Oh, it's a name, but not my name. "No," I tell him, "that's not us." Our phone service is in my husband's name, and I spell it for him. We repeat this step a few times, before moving on to the telephone number. Yes, that is our current number; yes, I am sure of my name. He apologizes politely for the error, and asks if I would like my telephone number changed anyway. No thanks, I've finally memorized the one we already have. We hang up. Somewhere in Hong Kong, a customer is calling the phone company, wanting to know what's happened to her new phone number.

And somewhere on an island, the Cayman Islands, I believe, a government bureaucrat is fuming at the Australian businessman who skipped town, dodging some sort of annual tax. I know because he called here looking for the scoundrel. His phone message was waiting for me when I came home one afternoon, shortly after we had arrived in Hong Kong, and although it made little sense, it did make me nervous. Could I please call a Mr. Peter Tam, it was urgent, the financial matter had to be settled, the interest rate on the amount due was about to double. I called Mr. Tam. As always, the language struggle. He was pleasant, but insistent. We owed the fee on our property, and we owed the annual registration fee for our business. I was having trouble understanding who he was, who he worked for, what property and what business he was referring to.

We persevered. Could it be that my husband and I owed some kind of tax on our apartment? Did the company that employed my husband miss a crucial payment of some sort? I spelled our names a number of times: was he sure he had the right number, the right deadbeats? He took a deep breath, audibly collecting his patience, and started over again, slowly. This time, I was able to pick out a few more words. When he came to "island" and "Australian," it was my turn to take a deep breath of relief. Wrong family, yes I'm quite sure, please believe me, if we were Australian, or owned a business incorporated on an island, I would be among those in the know. "But isn't your phone number this Australian fellow's fax number?" he asked. The question defied response, and the conversation ended.

I expect more of these calls — an inevitable consequence of Hong Kong's transient and multi-lingual population — and expect to spend a good deal of time spelling my name.

Dancing with daisies

THE MUSIC BLASTED out of the flowerpot, all horns and a smattering of piano. Four artificial daisies rode up and down, and twirled around in slow circles on their sturdy plastic stems, a floral merry-go-round of sorts, neatly contained in a small white pot. Two wobbling black and orange bumblebees were along for the ride, attached by a tiny sliver of wire to the gaily-colored petals. The flowers — or rather, the sudden onset of *In the Mood* — had stopped my slow progress through the narrow and jam-packed aisles of one of Hong Kong's Toys"R"Us stores. The music was tinny and slightly warbled, but unmistakable: accompanied by the flowerpot, the daisies were doing a stiff-stemmed dance to Glen Miller's big band swing-time classic. I put my search for finger-paints on hold, and gave this odd, motion-activated toy my full attention as the saxophones smoked through the famous refrain.

My timing was shot in any case; the store was packed, and I had given up hope of finding what I needed with quick efficiency. I am not a good shopper. Crowds confuse and annoy me, too many choices throw me, and more than once I have abandoned my selections at the sight of serpentine checkout lines. So I had planned this trip cautiously, knowing that a visit to this super-sized toy store would be particularly tricky no matter which shopping mall, American or Chinese, happens to house it. The scene is nearly always the same — frantically excited children and their exasperated parents elbow their way through stacks of toys, tussling over what gets picked up, what gets put back, what goes into the enormous shopping carts, and ultimately what gets bought, an exhausting battle of wills that can unnerve every adult within earshot. Kids shriek, parents try not to, toy weapons of every description rattle and spurt, play phones ring, mice, rabbits, puppies and kittens take turns squeaking, bleating, barking and meowing to the tune of *Ba Ba Black Sheep,* battery-powered action figures march around in mad configurations. Credit cards and checking accounts blister as cash registers total extraordinary sales. An effective form of birth control, perhaps, but nothing that anyone would want to repeat with regularity.

Tuesday, I decided, was the safest day of the week for my planned blitzkrieg. Weekend visits are suicide. Thursday and Friday, because of their proximity to Saturday and Sunday, were also out of the question. Mondays are grim enough as is. And I like Wednesdays too much to give over even one to masses of toys. Tuesday won by default. I chose eleven o'clock in the morning, hoping that other shoppers would find it an inconvenient hour to leave the house with small children — it is too close to lunchtime and an afternoon nap. My list was short: art supplies for my toddler, a bottle cleaner and pint-sized nail clippers for the baby, and as always, diapers. I promised myself that if I stayed focused, and did not let either the enormity of the store or the bilingual signs hanging over the aisles befuddle me, I could be in and out in half an hour; forty-five minutes, tops.

I was wrong.

The tour group is the first obstacle. I count seventeen children, pre-schoolers in matching orange tee-shirts, marching through the store entrance, book-ended by two teachers with whistles hanging from cords around their necks. To my astonishment, another group soon clusters at the door, shouting, waving, pushing, poking, grasping and clutching at each other, at their coins and bills, and of course, at the dollar-items lining the entryway, priced to move. I look over to watch the scene as the store employees catch wind of what is happening. Nothing. Two of them glance up, then back down at their registers with hardly a pause; one offers assistance, taking over as tour guide.

Nonplussed, I try to outdistance them, which I do, but I also get lost. I don't mean turned around, I mean outright lost. Can't find the exit, can't find the entrance. Certainly can't find the finger-paints. The Thunder Stinger with Spinning Lighting Bolt Energizer and the Storm Trooper Space Capsule look increasingly familiar — boxes and boxes of both toys are stacked the length of the dead-end aisle that I cannot seem to escape. I back out past the Mega-Sonic Crash Air

Hockey, and stumble across a section full of children climbing on jungle gyms, bouncing on miniature trampolines, and whooshing down slides, giving each piece of merchandise a full-out durability test. One little boy, legs pumping furiously, head bowed in concentration, takes his sister for a joy ride on the back of a bicycle, a streak of day-glo purple, first startling, then scattering shoppers. A group of Filipina nannies sit along the edge of the bottom shelf of the display racks, relaxing and chatting with each other. I suspect they come often.

A tingling behind my eyes warns of a headache. I find the paints, stop to take comfort in a sixty-four pack of crayons, sitting, it seems to me, with quiet dignity on a small shelf, and give up on the rest of my shopping list. I walk back past the daisies, looking sadly out of place among the sophisticated talking dolls, the cuddly dancing bears, the toys that will teach a child the alphabet, how to count, or the Mandarin language. The flowers are dear and uncomplicated, tacky, improbable, and finally, irresistible.

They sit, now, on my writing desk. When I'm stuck, tired or just bored, I wave my hand across the motion sensor on the pot, striking up the band, and take a turn around the room, dancing with my daisies.

Cheerios

IT'S THE PLASTIC BAGGIES full of Cheerios that throw me. There are other, more omnipresent signs of the curious zigzag that my life has become — diapers and bottles competing for space in my purse with a cell phone and pager, work clothes spotted with breast milk, time stolen from a job, a book, a project, to watch my daughters sleep — but none that wield the unnerving power of a baggie full of Cheerios.

I am living a stereotype, I think to myself each time I tuck the zippered bag into my pocket, knowing that I am one of legions of mothers toting around the cereal as a talisman of sorts against the bewildering, unpredictable temper tantrums of a one-year-old. If I'm not diligent, the stereotype, fed by television ads and sitcoms, parenting magazines and an over-active imagination, will tromp through my brain with a will of its own, overrunning long held and closely cherished beliefs about who and what I am, and replace them with a new portrait that I can hardly bear: a mother driving a mini-van, a mother attending PTA meetings, a mother arranging play dates, a mother whose free time is divided equally, and happily, between laundry, grocery shopping, and house keeping. This mother, she's made of molded plastic: no sharp edges, no surprises. Safe, contained, efficient. This mother, she makes no time for, indeed takes no notice of the me that existed before her.

But I don't begrudge her presence altogether. Crack her surface, and there I am in some of the smaller, less defined fragments, fragments that I suspect link me in more honest and fundamental ways to the hundreds of millions of mothers that have come before me. These fragments almost defy words — they are instead made up of slivers of instinct, deep, strong currents of new-found emotions, small sips of the giddy miracle of life. These fragments, when I can catch hold of them, leave me drunk with vulnerability.

Vulnerable, and naked to myself. No longer entirely familiar with the person that I have become. I do know this: my sense of self does not come in big, seemingly unassailable chunks any longer. Driven, ambitious, independent — not too long ago, I could comfortably hang out with these words, secure that they captured something true about me, something that I could fall back on when things got shaky. They were like my favorite pair of Levi's, softened in all of the right places from years of wear, but tough enough to lend a bit of swagger to my days.

I still work hard at keeping up a bit of that bravado. I like how it feels, and the license it grants me to move through the world with a certain impunity. But there's no swagger in stretch pants and maternity bras. There's nothing driven about the hours I spend coaxing a giggle out of my daughters. Nothing ambitious about breast-feeding. And precious little independence to be found within the new, complex matrix of my growing family.

I know this as well: the locus of my sense of self is slipping down from my head to my body. I had worked for years to keep a sizable portion of it lodged in my brain, sharpened by ideas, refined by words. Now, I find it flourishing in the circle of my arms, the fullness of my breasts, the roundness of my uterus. And I like it. I like it a lot more than I'm comfortable admitting just yet.

It's bewildering, this new portrait that's taking shape, and one that can make me panic about what I fear has been painted over. But there is a beauty as well in the fresh canvas, and a promise of gifts to come that I am learning to cherish.

Gweilo moments

THE CHINESE GOVERNMENT has officially noted that my husband's color is "weak." I would have to agree — Bill's mid-America, Wyoming-white skin does looks a bit laundered compared to the richer hues of Asian skin (the Chinese call a Caucasian expatriate *gweilo,* or "ghost person"). Still, I was surprised to see this peculiar reference to his pallor documented on a health certificate. It could be that Bill was paler than usual during the physical exam required of all foreigners who work in China: the procedures used by the employees at the state-run clinic to measure his health seemed designed instead to crack it. One nurse took his pulse by stripping him down to his underwear and attaching electrodes to his ankles and chest. Another nurse, fumbling with the task of drawing blood, stabbed a thick needle into a vein and plunged a syringe full of air directly into his bloodstream. Dazed by thoughts of embolisms, he did not protest a spine X-ray that irradiated his entire unprotected, underwear-clad body. Bill brought his health certificate home and, amused by my puzzlement over the "color: weak" notation, held off explaining that the reference was to his vision. Bill is partially color-blind.

On another occasion, during a chaotic early morning breakfast scene that included hungry children and visiting in-laws, I glanced at a headline in the *South China Morning Post,* the newspaper of record for the English-speaking community in Hong Kong, and caught something about executed pirates. My obligations to toast, peanut butter, bananas, coffee, wet-wipes, bibs, and spilt milk were momentarily abandoned as I tried to register this sentence fragment. Pirates? In Hong Kong?

The story, filed from Shanwei, in the province of Shanghai, was stranger even than the headline. "Thirteen pirates staggered drunkenly to their deaths," wrote reporter Michael Wong, "cursing the Communist Party and singing a Ricky Martin song." (Ricky Martin,

I later learned, is a Puerto Rican pop singer-sensation.) The gang members, as Wong called them, were convicted of murdering twenty-three crewmen on board the *Cheung Son,* a Hong Kong–registered cargo ship that was carrying thousands of tons of furnace slag from Shanghai to Malaysia. The pirates, who boarded the boat dressed as customs and public security officers, "beat the crew to death and dumped the bodies in the South China Sea after ten days on the vessel."

Before being led to the firing squad, the thirteen men were locked in the courtroom with their relatives, plates of food, and plenty of rice wine. Wong's story continues: "Half an hour later, they emerged unsteadily into bright sunlight strapped up ready for their executions, red in the face, shouting and singing. Six or seven of the pirates burst into a rendition of Ricky Martin's World Cup 1998 theme song *La copa de la vida* — or *The Cup of Life* — as they were loaded onto a truck outside the court." A short time later they were dead, killed by bullets fired to the head and heart, according to a "source close to the squad."

The brutality of the crime, the brutality of the execution, and the element of absurdity have given this story a certain staying power. It comes to mind when I have what I call a *gweilo* moment: an instant of cultural confusion that can be as insignificant as misunderstanding "color: weak," or as indicative of the chasm between the Western way of life and that of the Chinese as was the execution of thirteen drunken pirates. That the chasm is bridged everyday, time and time again in Hong Kong, is indisputable; that the bridge is occasionally illusory is also indisputable. It is part of what makes living in this city thrilling.

It is mid-March, and the streets of Hong Kong are beginning to thicken with tourists. The travel industry is big business here: the overlay of British influence on an Asian city makes Hong Kong an easy and appealing sell. Western tourists with limited appetite for adventure can visit a world-class Chinese city without leaving behind a single amenity — high tea for the British, coffee and scrambled eggs for the Americans, street signs, bus routes, and menus printed in English, convenience stores supplied with familiar brands of toothpaste and deodorant, hotel rooms with well-stocked mini-bars, firm mattresses and ample hot water — the list is comforting and seemingly inexhaustible.

The same can be said of living in Hong Kong. Well-heeled expatriate communities flourish on the outskirts of the densely populated city centers, like attracting like into light-skinned enclaves that hold Asia at arm's length, and that prefer to sample the Chinese culture on a part-time basis, long enough, say, to dine on *dim sum,* or to shop for bargains at the outdoor markets.

To be fair, Chinese Hong Kong can be politely enigmatic even while inviting the world to its doorstep. The only easy read is the stunning visual montage with its suggestion of the exotic for which the city is rightly famous: the ferries, fishing boats, container vessels and tugs crowding the harbor; the miles of fluorescent neon signs fixed one on top of another, a tightly packed, aggressive jumble of Chinese and English advertising arching out across the streets; the ubiquitous bamboo scaffolding that supports the multitude of construction projects continually underway; the ancestor shrines and medicine shops. It is a rich, tantalizing physical environment and one that adroitly conceals the layered secrets of a deeply traditional lifestyle behind a seemingly transparent façade.

The only sure-fire way to reach across boundaries is to enter the world of commerce: if Hong Kong is about any one thing, it is about money, and the ability to turn a quick buck trumps most other considerations. Nimbleness pays off here; those who do best in Hong Kong have a cultural dexterity that allows them to wear their nationality loosely.

My own abilities in this arena are as yet rudimentary, and although I am not as flat-footed as some, I have often blundered when a light step was called for. One such misstep nearly cost our Filipina nanny her work visa. Yolly and I had gone together to the eighth floor of the Department of Immigration, where we hoped to put an end to a series of frustrating delays that had held up her work visa for months. It was her third appointment, and Yolly had asked me to come along this time, hoping that the presence of her prospective employer would help speed the process.

We stepped off the elevator into a crowded waiting room where dozens of Filipinas sat waiting for their names to be called, their usually lively conversations muted by anxiety. They had much at stake

— despite the long hours and difficult working conditions they endure as domestic helpers (a bureaucratic euphemism since many, if not most, are treated like servants), the wages, while ludicrously low by Hong Kong standards, are equivalent to white-collar wages in the Philippines, and many of the women renew their two-year employment contracts several times over.

When Yolly's turn came, she and I began handing over reams of paperwork to the immigration officer. I explained that we had completed all of the required forms — in fact, we had completed them three separate times for three separate appointments, and as he could see (Sera and Natalie, bored by the wait, were barely under control), I needed help with child-care before I could resume my own work. He was polite but uninterested in my speech. He took his stamps and rubber bands away from my toddler and began asking questions that were clearly answered in the thick file he was studying.

"Where will your helper be living?" he asked.

"She has a room in a boarding house, and my husband and I will be responsible for the rent," I answered.

"Why not live with you?" he wanted to know. Growing annoyed at the repetition of information, I pointed to the written explanation in the stack of documents — our apartment was too small to accommodate a domestic helper — and, I added, the room designed as living quarters for a domestic helper was not fit to live in. It was hardly bigger than a closet, with no window, no ventilation, no heating nor air-conditioning. He continued pressing the point until finally I pressed back.

"We've been through this before. What's the problem here?"

"Look," he said, "I just don't believe you. Your apartment is twice as big as most apartments in Hong Kong. Government workers live with our families in 400 square foot flats. I would be glad to have your helper's room."

He was right. Housing in Hong Kong is outrageously expensive and cramped, and our relatively spacious apartment suddenly embarrassed me. Still, I did not understand why the Department of Immigration cared where Yolly lived. He continued, "If we're not very strict, all of the domestic helpers would take rooms in a boarding house."

"And why is that a problem?" I asked.

"Because then they would have their freedom," he answered. In the ensuing silence, I began to understand just how badly I had misjudged the situation. Every detail of the contract Yolly and I had negotiated offended this man: the above-average wages, the American-style work schedule, the benefits package, the living arrangements — evidence, all of it, that I regarded Yolly as a professional and accorded her respect, a perspective wildly at odds with his own.

We sat, the three of us, across a divide of race, class, gender, and nationality and considered the impasse: the immigration officer quiet, waiting, Yolly angry and offended, and myself, stunned and fearful that the meeting could end with an order for deportation. I could not think of a way to abrogate Yolly's rights on paper without abrogating them in actuality, nor could I pretend to have a spontaneous change of heart, shedding my middle-class, liberal-minded American sensibility as if I had suddenly realized it was the wrong size, and wrapping myself instead in something more appropriate for the occasion — we had gone too far for that. The locus of power in our triad, which I had naively assumed we shared, was now clearly and irrevocably concentrated in the hands of the immigration officer, and perhaps for that reason he abruptly yielded and showed us how to amend the contract to make it acceptable to him and presumably the Department of Immigration. We made the changes, each of us signing a fresh stack of documents and concluded our business in near silence.

It is tempting to chalk up the many conflicts, misunderstandings, and misperceptions that arise among the residents of Hong Kong to cultural differences and leave it there, but that loads the concept of culture with more freight than it was originally intended to carry. There is more at play than a clash of languages, values, life experiences, and nationalities. What it comes down to is this: we live in different worlds. The Filipina domestic helpers, the native Chinese residents, the newly arrived immigrants from all over the globe — we might meet up at the grocery store, at the bank, in office buildings, even in private homes, but beyond these easily accessed, shared points of reference, we have constructed such wholly different worlds for ourselves that they cannot plausibly be reduced to the one real, true, fixed world of Hong Kong. Overlap and intersection happen along the periphery, not at the core. Multiple domains flourish, and reductionism, no matter how far one takes it, will not yield an inviolate set of common denominators.

This is not an original claim. For decades (centuries even, if one frames the questions and issues broadly enough) it has been the subject of contentious debate among philosophers. When I first came across the concept a few years ago, it threw me, for I had an unquestioned belief in the "real" world. That it shared characteristics both trivial and profound with the world as known by others seemed self-evident, as did the fact that I might recognize very little of the world as experienced by millions of others. Still, the fact that I had no idea what kind of life a Chinese rice farmer might lead did not in any way suggest to me that we inhabited different worlds in a *literal* sense. We might have radically different experiences, or similar experiences to which we assigned radically different meanings, but the world was the world — firm, solid, real.

So what to make of the claims by a generation of philosophers that the world is not as it seems; that truth, regardless of what it is applied to — a particular world-view, science, history, human nature — is made, not found; that fact and fiction are nourished — sometimes well, sometimes badly — by each other?

It is a tangled and disquieting set of questions, which makes the confidence and surety of two of the leading philosophers in this field all the more remarkable. Nelson Goodman, a professor of philosophy at Harvard University, is not a household name by any stretch of the imagination; nevertheless, some of his ideas have seeped into popular consciousness. Ever heard someone say about the bizarre guy living next door, "what planet is *he* from?" It's a Goodman-esque question. Goodman, in *Ways of Worldmaking*, places his work in the context of a philosophical movement away from "unique truth and a world fixed and found to a diversity of right and even conflicting versions or worlds in the making." His first task is to pry his readers loose from our bedrock belief in a singular world, and here he wastes few words, arguing that for the man-in-the-street what passes for reality is nothing more or less than the "familiar serviceable world he has jerry-built from fragments of scientific and artistic tradition and from his own struggle for survival. This world, indeed is the one most often taken for real; for reality in a world, like realism in a picture, is largely a matter of habit." A physicist may have a more sophisticated, more learned construction; an artist may have a more impressionistic construction; both of them may take their world for real in the same way as does the man-in-the-street.

But taking something for real does not mean it *is* real. What Goodman proposes instead is a multiplicity of worlds and "world-versions," arguing that our perception of reality depends on our frame of reference. What's more, this multiplicity of worlds cannot be reduced to a single "right world" version from which all other versions spring. There is no "neutral *something* beneath these versions," Goodman writes, and indeed he believes that the idea of a firm foundation is an idea well lost.

Goodman is hardly alone in this. Richard Rorty, one of contemporary philosophy's most provocative thinkers, lays out a similar argument in *Contingency, Irony and Solidarity.* While acknowledging that the world is "out there," (that is, existing in time and space independent of human mental conceptions) Rorty agrees with Goodman that we have no way to ascertain the truth about the world — what it is or is not, what perspective or frame of reference captures its essence, or which set of facts and theories about the world are true or false. Key to this argument is his belief that nothing — not "mind or matter, self or world" — has an intrinsic nature that can be revealed (or found) by the right set of analytical or metaphysical tools. Our beliefs about the "right" world (and human nature) are simply a matter of contingency, created by a random combination of historical, cultural, and personal circumstances.

This creates a bit of a mess. If we agree to travel along the theoretical road set out by Goodman and Rorty (among others) and accept the multiplicity of worlds and the contingencies by which they are created, then we are left with badly mauled concepts of truth and reality. Neither philosopher offers much comfort on the subject. Goodman says of truth that it "is often inapplicable, is seldom sufficient, and must sometimes give way to competing criteria." Truth, in other words, is not an entirely useless concept, but it certainly does not deserve its exalted position within our contemporary society. It is relative; the truth that fits one world-version may be proved false when measured against a different world-version. Truth, then, cannot be conceived of as having a one-to-one correspondence with the "real" world.

Rorty, with his emphasis on the critical role language and vocabulary play in creating our frames of reference, helps clarify this perspective. "To say that the truth is not out there," he argues, "is simply to say that where there are no sentences there is no truth, that sentences are elements of human languages, and that human languages are human creations." This is a tightly packed claim. To back up a bit, remember that Rorty does not deny that the, or *a*, world actually exists. But we have no way to gauge what is true or false about that world because we cannot gain a privileged perspective beyond our created language from which we can objectively measure the world. "The world is out there, but descriptions of the world are not." So where does this leave truth? Or questions about how to distinguish between true and false worlds? For Rorty, these are questions best put aside, since there is little point in pressing for an answer that will at best be true or false only under a particular set of contingent circumstances.

Neither Goodman nor Rorty mean to suggest that anything goes — that scientific enquiry, for example, has no stake in proving or disproving hypotheses. We can expect that engineers will get it "right" when they calculate the weight-bearing load of a 747 airplane, or that a brain surgeon operating on a patient has a "correct" understanding of anatomy, and can identify the "wrong-ness" of a tumor from the "rightness" of healthy tissue. But it is unlikely that today's seemingly unassailable truths will remain unchanged and unchallenged over time; we have only to look at the history of science to be reminded that new paradigms are most often built on the ruins of old ones.

To return to Goodman's description of the man-in-the-street jerry-built world: the everyday worlds that most of us take for real are not illusions — when we put our feet down, we hit solid ground underneath. That our understanding of them is con-structed from a set of contingent circumstances, or stitched together from bits and pieces of mediated experience, does not necessarily make them any less serviceable. But it does mean that we must stop asking of these worlds, "Are they true?" Nowhere is this more obvious than in an unfamiliar country. The answers are not forthcoming; the *gweilo* moments are reminders that reality is as wobbly as jello. Ricky Martin and pirates can slip into my world at the breakfast table. An encounter with an immigration officer affords me an unexpected glimpse into an unfamiliar universe, as does talking with Yolly over a cup of coffee. There are advantages to this. A concrete, fixed reality slaps a label on incoming experience — right or wrong, true or false, black or white — and files it away. A malleable reality provides ample room to reconsider how one's particular world is structured and whether or not it might bear expansion. It grants us the freedom to suspend judgment, if only temporarily, in favor of taking a close look around.

Going the distance with these philosophical concepts requires, as Richard Rorty puts it, turning away from a search for overarching truths about "an order beyond time and change." "Such a turn," he concludes, "would be emblematic of our having given up the attempt to hold all the sides of our life in a single vision, to describe them with a single vocabulary." While I have to knock the concept down any number of levels in order to be able to grab it off the shelf, I am inclined to give it a try.

Hardware

VISITORS FROM HOME often ask me what I miss about living in the States. "K-Mart," I answer, facing down their incredulous stares. I explain: real estate in Hong Kong is a precious commodity and, as a consequence, super-sized stores filled with aisle upon aisle of merchandise are largely unheard of here. Instead, each neighborhood spawns hundreds of small, specialized shops squeezed into narrow alleys and side streets, many of which can only be found by word of mouth. This makes shopping something of an adventure for newcomers. My first trip to the grocery store should have tipped me off. I could find produce, bread, and dairy products, but nothing else. Odd, I thought. Wonder where one buys toilet paper, rice, and beer? Turns out there is a tiny staircase in a back corner of the store artfully hidden behind racks of white bread and hamburger buns that leads down to a small basement full of non-perishable products. I did not make this discovery on my own, much to my embarrassment.

I have since thoroughly canvassed my neighborhood memorizing the location of shops that look useful. I found the stapler, note pads, tape dispenser, and copy paper for my office; I found a mop, a broom, and a dustpan; I found diaper cream, baby bibs, plastic plates, insect spray, and my favorite brand of pain reliever; I found a toilet plunger, a new ink cartridge for the computer printer, extension cords, and a transformer. I found each of these items at different stores, and I also found shopping, one of my least favorite activities, swallowing up enormous chunks of time.

It was with some trepidation, then, that I set off one Saturday morning to buy a can of paint and a couple of paintbrushes. My best hope was a rather strange little hardware store just a few blocks from home. This store is quintessentially Hong Kong. It is extremely small with narrow, tightly packed aisles. The shelves bulge with an eccentric mix of merchandise arranged seemingly at random. (My favorite display is the stack of cushioned toilet seats, which rests upon a stack of cushioned pet beds.)

The shopkeeper, a small, efficient, Chinese woman with a reputation for knowing the name and function of every imaginable piece of hardware, meets me at the threshold. "Yes?" It is not an invitation to browse. I explain that I need some paint and try to squeeze my way past her to the back of the store. I'd like to study my options. I'm not sure if I want a flat finish or a semi-gloss, an oil-based paint or a water-based paint. The basic color is easy — white — but I have some questions about shades and hues. I want to read the back of the cans, study the color charts, do a bit of comparison-shopping.

"You paint what?" the shopkeeper asks. She is already stacking cans of paint on the counter next to the cash register.

"A bed frame," I tell her, and she takes back the can I had picked up. "Color?"

"White," I answer with a sigh of resignation, as it has become clear that she is in charge of the decision making. One can is pushed forward; the others are whisked away. "Brushes?" I ask.

"There," she points behind me.

"Thinner?" I say, trying to keep the monosyllabic rhythm going. She bends down behind the counter, plucks a bottle of beer from the floor, sets it down in front of me, and starts adding up my purchases. I stare at the beer, stupefied. It is a corked bottle of San Miguel, an inexpensive and popular brand of beer sold in nearly every grocery store and restaurant in Hong Kong. But why here and why now?

My brain clicks through any number of explanations, each one more absurd than the last, before I hit on the answer: this glass bottle is full of turpentine, paint thinner. My bewilderment is obvious, and the shopkeeper takes advantage of this to shoo me out the door. Walking home, I contemplate my purchases, for which I paid approximately five dollars: one can of paint labeled entirely in Chinese, two medium-sized paint brushes selected for me with no more than a passing reference to the size of the paint job, and one Molotov cocktail. Perhaps it's time to re-think my shopping preferences. K-Mart may be more practical, but it will never be this much fun.

The switch

THE LOCKER ROOM attendant was standing so close that I couldn't help bumping her with knees and elbows as I stepped into my bathing suit. She had spotted me the instant I came down the steps into the changing room, carrying Sera in one arm and my gym bag in the other, and was on my heels in a flash, giggling and chattering non-stop in Cantonese. She took me by the elbow and showed me the showers, the toilets, and the well-marked, hard-to-miss entrance to the swimming pool. I understood from her gestures that I was to use the locker she had chosen for me, and I let her pull my gym bag from my shoulder and stuff it upside down into the locker to demonstrate how the process worked. Nodding and smiling, I tugged it out again to retrieve bathing suits, towels, sunscreen, and a swim diaper, and, trying to match her enthusiasm, thanked her in Cantonese, thanked her in English, and thanked her in Mandarin, hoping that one of the thank-yous would break through the one-way language barrier and signal to her that I would be okay on my own now, *mm goy,* thank you, *xiexie.*

It was pointless, and I knew it. She was going to supervise the whole shebang. Modesty was not at issue — this happened each time I brought the kids swimming, and I had become accustomed to changing into my bathing suit so closely surrounded by helpful strangers that I could easily end up with spare body parts caught in the straps of my suit. Practicality was an issue. It's tough trying to change a squirming toddler on a narrow, wet, slick-tiled bench, and even tougher if she is the object of much curiosity. Extra hands in this situation could prove useful, but only if they were well-disciplined, attached to my arms, and under my control. These hands were not; these hands wanted to finger Sera's light-brown, curly hair — a novelty, a curiosity, an oddity among the sheets of straight black hair being shampooed and shook out all around us.

The scene was much the same in the pool. Bill and Natalie, who had made it through the men's locker room quickly and without interruption, were easy to spot: they were the only Westerners in the pool (which is virtually always the case on our visits), and they were surrounded by a crowd (which is virtually always the case on our visits). In the locker room, it was the older women who comprised our audience, but in the pool, it was typically the teenage girls and parents of small children who vied for our attention. The teens took over entertaining Sera and Natalie and the parents pressed their children forward for an impromptu language lesson. Bill and I spoke our parts over and over again: "Hello," "How are you?" "I'm fine," and "Goodbye."

The children, anxious to get this recitation over with, would quickly duck under water or paddle away as soon as the last syllable left their lips, but their parents could not have looked more pleased, and would often linger for a slightly more advanced version of this *Dick and Jane*–style conversation. (No one paid any attention to me as I apologized for speaking hardly a word of Cantonese — it was English they wanted.) After an hour or so, when Bill and I began to feel the urge to make ourselves invisible, we plucked Natalie and Sera out of their circle of admirers and headed back to the locker rooms. This time, Bill took Sera, and I took Natalie.

The attendant looked stricken. She ran her hands over Natalie's head and then over her own, again gesturing (this time in agitation), and talking rapid-fire at my back as I made my way to a dry spot on the bench. Unsure of the problem, but not wanting to be rude, I held Natalie up for inspection, and said in my best everything-is-fine-no-need-to-worry public television voice, "She's fine, really, just wet, and in need of a clean diaper."

The attendant was not appeased, and off she went in search of someone who spoke English. The young woman who came back with her did her best. "What about your baby's hair?" she asked me. It was generous of her — Natalie has at best three or four wisps of light blond hair and I am the only one who won't concede her baldness. "Yes, I know," I answered, "she doesn't have much hair, but what she does have is growing, and there will be more to come, I'm sure."

"But do you cut it?" the young woman asked, egged on by the attendant.

"Huh?"

"Do you cut it at the pool?"

"Do I cut it at the pool?" I repeated, confused.

By now, I understood the gestures: the attendant was grasping handfuls of her own hair and pretending to cut it. Was she trying to tell me that it was against the rules to get a poolside hair cut? That seemed fair enough. "Okay," I said, nodding my consent.

The young woman tried again. "Where's the hair?"

I got it. I suddenly got it. The attendant thought Natalie was Sera, and was accusing me of chopping off her curls. The thought of lopping off chunks of hair as Sera innocently floated by in the baby pool made me laugh. "No, no," I said, "this isn't the same baby. My other child is with her father. She still has all of her hair." Blank looks all around. "I have two children. Sera has lots of hair. Natalie doesn't. This is Natalie, not Sera." This was not working. I was ready to give it up, and more importantly, so was Natalie-not-Sera, who wanted her bottle, *right now before I start screaming, please.* Our hair-cutting scene was played out, and I turned my attention to finding the baby formula and getting dressed. As the attendant wandered off, I'm sure she was muttering, "They all look alike to me."

The quickening

ROM THE MOMENT of conception, I knew that the love I would
feel for my children would be unparalleled. I had read it in
countless books, and heard it from nearly every parent I encountered.
I readily believed it: my first daughter was hardly more than a
collection of cells, multiplying fast, laying down the microscopic
blueprint for the work of the next nine months, and already I was
fiercely protective of her. I wept when I first heard her heartbeat, and
again when I first felt her move against my belly. But writers far more
gifted than I have struggled to describe the love a parent feels for a
child, and I leave it to them to convey the enormity of it. What has
stunned me is the fear: a visceral, primal fear that hollows out my
heart; a fear that no book, nor any friend, could have prepared me
for, a fear that momentarily strips me of reason. It is, in its largest
manifestation, a terror of the dangers that could rip my children from
me.

I understand its germination: it quickens as life quickens. Like
countless other women, I fretted over the real and the imagined
complications of both of my pregnancies, the early bouts of bleeding,
the possibility of birth defects, the long hours when the babies rested,
still and unresponsive to my probes. The worst of it, I was sure, would
pass with the birth of a healthy child. And much of it did. But what
lingered of it has eaten from a black spot in my imagination. The local
newspaper picks up a wire story about six girls, neighborhood playmates, who climb into the trunk of a car to play on a hot summer
day. They suffocate. All of them. A former colleague of mine goes for
a job interview with a child-protection agency in Chicago and tells
me about the father who falls asleep in the bathtub with his baby. The
child drowns. Our nanny in Hong Kong tells me about family friends
searching the streets of China for their kidnapped son. They find him,
but what has happened to him in the intervening time makes me sick

to my stomach. And I wonder: do all parents play out these stories in their heads, over and over again, projecting the image of their child into the middle of someone else's tragedy? Do others lie awake at night, imagining fires and car accidents, bombings, plane crashes, and abductions — or even the horrific consequences of a simple moment of inattention? How many of us rehearse our rescues and plot escape routes hoping to trick fate and forestall catastrophe? What will it take, what must I do, to wrap an impenetrable envelope of protection around my children? I am desperate for an answer.

My fears are wildly, outrageously, out of proportion to the kinds of commonplace dangers my children face. I know that, but knowledge does little to blunt their power. They are, it seems, as deeply rooted as my love — and maybe that's how it has to be. Profound love inexorably twisted and bound up with the specter of profound loss, each fed from the same source, neither answering to analysis, calculation, or rational understanding. It is trite to say that my job is to learn to let my children find their own way in the world, knowing that I cannot fully shelter them. So here's where I begin: my job, I think, is to learn to trust that this relationship is interdependent, that the depth of the fear highlights the depth of the love, and to nurture a faith that the love will check the fear and keep me from holding my children so close, and protecting them so furiously, that I squeeze the life out of them.

Menopause, mid-life, and motherhood

DR. SINCLAIR STANDS UP and absent-mindedly tugs at her underwear through the skirt of her sleeveless black linen dress. A note in my medical file has momentarily caught her attention, and while she gives it another look I take the opportunity to study her. Her dress is heavily creased across the lap and fits snuggly around her full hips and breasts. She is wearing a thick gold necklace with matching earrings and a sensible looking watch. Her chocolate-brown loopy curls look soft and inviting, and I check an impulse to reach out and tousle a handful.

As if catching my thought, she pushes her hand through her hair as she tells me, "Well, it looks like we were right — it's premature menopause. You'll need to come back in six to eight weeks so we can check your estrogen level again before starting you on hormone replacement therapy." She is British, and pronounces "estrogen," *eastrogen,* with a long *e.* I am off-balance and grab hold of a small contradiction to demonstrate competency: a few minutes ago she had told me to come back in three months. "Did I say three months? I'm going mad."

Her practice is full, and this morning the demands on her time are evident, but her gaze remains clear, direct, smart. Her slate-gray eyes meet mine — judging my reaction, I suppose, to the news she's just given me — and satisfied with what she sees, ends the appointment. In the cluttered hallway outside the exam room, a nurse is talking on the phone. She and Dr. Sinclair make a quick exchange: the nurse takes me to draw blood; Dr. Sinclair takes the phone and tells the caller, "I'll be there shortly. Keep her on her side."

I am familiar with the routine the nurse and I are about to slip into, and while she prepares a needle and vial, I roll up the sleeve of my blouse and rest my left arm on a small scarlet cushion. I've learned through experience that the veins in my right arm tend to collapse if probed too deeply with a needle, leaving the nurse without enough blood and me with a black and green bruise the size of a golf-ball. I've also learned to offer up a measured amount of chitchat to reassure the nurse that I'm not going to faint or make a fuss. In truth, I don't mind the procedure, and as my blood begins flowing through the clear plastic tube, I fall silent and ruminate on the turn of events that have led me to this moment.

My first visit to Dr. Sinclair's obstetrics and gynecology practice, situated on the 34th floor of a prestigious high-rise in the Wan Chai district, had come ten months earlier. My husband and I were trying for a third child, but my menstrual cycle had become erratic and ovulation virtually impossible to track. I saw one of Dr. Sinclair's colleagues on a friend's recommendation. Dr. Wilson had an understated, almost shy, way about him and took my medical history with a thoroughness that bordered on tedious. When the paperwork was complete, a nurse led me to a screened area of the exam room. While she and the doctor waited, I disrobed and, feeling like a gag gift at a bachelor's party, wrapped myself in a disposable paper gown. I left my socks on in an act of childish defiance — one that seemed less than necessary when I noticed the absence of the humiliating mounted stirrups that dominate gynecological exam rooms in the States.

After Dr. Wilson finished probing my uterus and ovaries with as much delicacy as is possible for such a rough physical task, we moved back to his desk for what I assumed was the heart of the visit. I was anticipating a talk about fertility and infertility, warnings about my age, miscarriage and potential birth defects, even some delicate second-guessing of our decision to try for a third child. I was feeling defensive about trying to conceive again and unaccountably ashamed of myself for my failure to pull it off. I was ready to overcompensate by diving into a lengthy discussion of the medical options open to my husband and me. Instead, Dr. Wilson handed me a month's supply of Clomid, a drug designed to induce ovulation, gave me brief instructions for taking the medication, and sent me back to the reception area to pay my bill.

I felt as guilty as a thief leaving the office. My husband and I had already made the decision not to get involved with complicated fertility treatments, but I knew that, despite our agreement, I was going to start on the Clomid. I took the elevator down to the first floor deli, sat with a cup of coffee and read what the manufacturer had to say about the drug.

Clomid is a brand name for clomiphene, and it works by telling one's pituitary gland to produce the hormones that trigger ovulation. Millions of women take clomiphene each year, and the success rate for this class of fertility drugs is reported to be quite high. I had been prescribed a low dose, and what I told my husband later that evening was true: it was just enough to help regulate my cycle, and the chance of multiple birth was only about two to five percent. What I wasn't ready to admit was that I had earlier made the agreement with him not to engage in fertility treatment because I did not for a minute think I might need it.

The Clomid did not work. I took it in increasing amounts for five months until it became excruciatingly clear that I was a statistical anomaly. My ovaries could not be cajoled into releasing an egg, and my husband, never wildly enthusiastic about a third biological child, gently signaled an end to his willingness to push the envelope. My failure — for I took it personally — drifted through me with a leeching sadness. Rationally, I knew that I was not prepared to take the next step in fertility treatment with its concurrent risk of multiple births and other complications; at the same time, I was dead certain that another child was meant to be born to me. Her name is Claire, and I can feel her weight in my arms, taste her soft breath. I wanted to believe that I could compel her into existence through force of will, make her tangible by the strength of my desire and certainty. She was — still is — quite real to me. How could I abandon her?

Here's how the psychiatrist explained it to me: Depression does not have a single cause. Instead, myriad causes are arrayed along a continuum. (My mind wanders. The depression takes on a doggy personality, lying limp on the floor, unable to summon the energy to snap to. It yawns and I smell its yellowed breath. I'd like to lie down as well and take a nap.) He continues: clustered at one end are the biological causes, at the other, the purely psychological causes. My case falls somewhere in the middle. (Boom. Silence.) A biological component is likely since depression has taunted me off and on since adolescence. Unresolved grief weighs in at the other end of the scale. I don't want to talk about it — he is too young, too fresh, shifts around too much in his well-tailored suit. I want a prescription, which I get. A month's supply of an anti-depressant, a blue plastic pill splitter, and an hour's consultation cost close to three hundred dollars. I hand over my credit card. Goddamned dog.

After I stopped taking the Clomid, I went months without a period, which finally prompted me to make another appointment at the clinic. An old, shopworn prejudice resurfaced, and I asked to see a woman. My appointment fell on a day soaked through by a hard, driving rain — predictable weather during the summer typhoon season — and in the early morning hours, the Hong Kong Observatory issued the latest in a string of flood, storm, and landslide warnings, this one serious enough to close down all schools and disrupt public transport. The rain also caused trouble for the ferry I take into town from my apartment on Lantau Island — something about clogged water-intake valves — and I arrived wet and fifteen minutes late for my appointment. The receptionist was uncharacteristically short with me when I checked in. "Dr. Sinclair is in a hurry this morning," she told me in a clipped voice. "She has a patient in labor." Partly chastised, partly annoyed, I dumped my dripping umbrella in the umbrella stand, found an empty seat and a battered fashion magazine, and began the wait.

When I am led into an exam room some twenty-five minutes later, Dr. Sinclair is already seated, flipping through my chart. It is a long moment before she looks up and nods hello. We introduce ourselves, and she returns her attention to the chart, poised to interpret the results of numerous blood tests telling of hormones missing and present. She asks about the Clomid, the details of my menstrual cycle over the past year, the anti-depressant, the infertility. "Are you still trying to get pregnant?" she asks. "No," I tell her, keeping it short, and concentrating on maintaining my composure. Someone opens the door to the exam room a few inches, closes it again softly.

Dr. Sinclair is younger than I had expected — late thirties, perhaps — and her manner is straightforward and confident. She tells me with a mock grimace that they are having computer trouble and that her kids, kept out of school by the rain, are with her at the office today. She also has a patient in labor. I nod, understanding that she is apologizing for the receptionist, the interruption, her own air of minor distraction. I am expecting this to be a routine visit, and I assume by her questions, mostly concerning my medical history over the past year, that she expects the same.

We are both surprised, then, when a casual remark hits an unexpected target and turns the conversation serious. She had been explaining the various causes of amenorrhoea — the medical term for interrupted menstruation — when she mentions that we could most likely rule out menopause because of my age and because I had not experienced hot flashes. "I've been having hot flashes for years," I tell her. She is clearly startled.

"Hot flashes are a strong indicator of menopause," she responds, with a question in her voice.

"I've had them since I was thirty-five, maybe even younger. In the last few months, I've been having them every night." I remember a recent flight from New York to Hong Kong. I spent what felt like the entire fifteen-hour trip pulling a black, loose-knit sweater over my head, off and on, off and on again, as my internal thermostat went on strike.

Dr. Sinclair listens closely, then rechecks my age — at forty-one, I am well shy of the average age for the onset of menopause, but the signs are there. I get a crash course in the decline of my reproductive process. Women of my mother's generation were led to believe that menopause was a singular event — *the change* — with a definitive beginning and end point. Instead, menopause is a process, and for some women, the onset can go unnoticed and the early stages continue for years.

It begins when a woman's ovaries start making less estrogen and progesterone — the hormones that regulate ovulation and menstruation. The first stage of menopause is called perimenopause, and I had apparently been experiencing this since my mid-to-late thirties. During perimenopause the levels of estrogen and progesterone fluctuate, rising and falling unevenly, and resulting in symptoms like hot flashes and irregular periods. The ovaries can still produce fertilized eggs, although not as readily, and I had twice become pregnant during this time. The second stage, postmenopause, is signaled by the absence of menstruation over a twelve-month period.

It is possible, Dr. Sinclair tells me, that my ovaries are "blinking in and out," meaning that I may not yet be fully menopausal. She will need to track my hormone levels for two or three more months to confirm a diagnosis, and to settle on treatment options. She asks me to schedule another appointment in one month's time and looks at me expectantly. I know she needs to end the appointment, so I ask no further questions.

The tube is full of bright red, healthy-looking blood. The nurse eases the needle out of my vein, ending my reverie, and hands me a cotton ball to press against the small wound. "There," she says, with a pronounced Scottish accent. "That's all we need." She is quick and proficient, and I am grateful. While I pay my bill at the front desk, she gathers brochures on hormone replacement therapy for me to take home and study, including, ironically, one that describes the "wider role" of an intrauterine device. I take a quick look through it and learn that I can be fitted with an IUD, which for a period of up to three years will prevent the conception of a baby I long for, and, as a side-benefit for the older (or confused) woman, will also slowly release the hormones necessary to manage the symptoms of menopause. I want to weep; instead, I politely thank her, sign my charge slip, and make my next appointment before escaping the clinic.

A friend recently sent me an Internet-originated joke that purports to list the delights of mid-life and menopause. *Mid-life is when the growth of hair on our legs slows down. This gives us plenty of time to care for our newly acquired mustache. In mid-life women no longer have upper arms, we have wingspans. We are no longer women in sleeveless shirts; we are flying squirrels in drag. Mid-life is when you can stand naked in front of a mirror and see your rear end without turning around. Mid-life is when you go for a mammogram and realize that it is the only time someone will ask you to appear topless on film.* Is this funny? I have lost my perspective (and, perhaps, my sense of humor). I find the joke disorienting; it is about me, and yet it is not. There is no denying that I have entered mid-life: menopause is my membership card. But this is not the sort of joke that would circulate among the parents of pre-schoolers (much less would-be pregnant women): wrong demographic altogether.

I can often see this apparent contradiction about where I fit in reflected in the faces of my acquaintances. A few days ago, Natalie, now two, announced to the mother of a playmate that I had just celebrated a birthday and had turned forty-two. The woman laughed and shook her head at me as if to say, "kids — you never know what will come out of their mouths." I didn't have the heart to tell her that Natalie was reporting the facts correctly. Imagine her reaction if she knew the whole story.

And so it is that with lightning speed menopause and its tangle of implications has knotted itself around me like kudzu, leaving me unexpectedly shaken. My initial response was absurd. I stubbornly insisted that the changes wrought by my irregular supply of hormones were exclusively physical and did not have the power to launch me into a morbid and anti-feminist period of mourning over the loss of youthful femininity. I bristled at the suggestion that menopause might be a factor, however small, in my recent depression. I dredged up, then fought off, every cruel and ignorant stereotype of post-menopausal women I had ever run across.

Gradually, though, the initial surge of fight-'em-to-the-finish adrenaline drained away, and I had to admit that I felt diminished by Dr. Sinclair's diagnosis, as if her words had effected the change rather than simply named a process that had been going on for years. I called my mother for reassurance. She, too, had been surprised by premature menopause (daughters tend to follow their mothers quite closely in this regard, I have since learned), and we spent a long while on the phone comparing notes about the genetically influenced parallels between our biological histories. We had both gone gray in our early thirties, developed the first smattering of age spots and arthritis not much later, and had crossed into our forties with menopause at our heels.

But despite these and other similarities in our aging process, my mother and I stand at opposite ends of a unique generation gap. My siblings and I were teenagers when my mother went through menopause. She had stopped thinking about babies a decade and a half before her body reached a similar conclusion. For many women of my mother's generation, this span was even more exaggerated. On average, women now in their late sixties and seventies gave birth in their mid-twenties. Their children were grown — or nearly so — by the time menopause set in. For some (and this was true of my mother) menopause came as a relief — no more periods to deal with. Good riddance, my mother harrumphed more than once. On that score, I have to agree. But what am I to do with this: I confused symptoms of menopause with symptoms of pregnancy. Over the course of five or six months, I spent a small fortune on home pregnancy tests, believing that my mood swings and missed periods signaled the waxing, rather than the waning, of fertility. By what act of grace did I conceive two babies even while my reproductive system was shutting down?

I, and a virtual army of others like me, have put the squeeze on biology (or is it the other way around?) by delaying childbirth. It is not that we want it all (that dreadful, facile observation-*cum*-accusation carelessly tossed about like confetti) — it's that we want to mess with the time-line. Mid-life and motherhood, each lugging around their own set of burdensome images and expectations, are tripping over each other in unprecedented ways, not only sharing space in the same house, but sharing the same bed. *That certain age* is no longer so certain.

If I could single-handedly recast the images of mid-life (as I am struggling to do for myself, at least), the first thing I would do is sever it from images of decay. This is not about sagging breasts or spreading hips. The stereotypes are neither funny nor wry; they strip us of our sexuality, our sensuality, our pleasure in our bodies, our visibility as women. I adamantly refuse to relinquish any of these qualities.

Moreover, I will not be nudged from center-stage of my own life by outdated (though tenacious) ideas about how an older woman is supposed to behave. This is about power. Evolution tells us that our job is done once our children are relatively self-sufficient. Menopause was intended as a pink slip. Forget it. Reject it. Make *that* the joke. Accrue power through experience. Define it for yourself, and gather it to you as a right and a reward of a hard-won maturity. Cede this to no one — certainly not to the whims and vagrancies of pop culture, consumerism, or the mass media, each of which has an enormous stake in telling us who we are, what we look like, and how we act.

These are the broad strokes. The details are difficult to fill in because they have not yet been fully created, and we have little to go on. I notice, though, women of my age and older watching their peers — not with the edgy competitiveness of a twenty-something, but with genuine interest and regard. We are looking to see how other women wear a seasoned femininity, what it looks like and how it walks through the world. We take the details and tuck them away, like magpies gathering bright treasures for a nest, resolutely building something that fits the circumstances of our lives.

I have made one further visit to see Dr. Sinclair. She prescribed a low-dose hormone replacement therapy — or HRT, as it is commonly called — and I started it with few qualms, since, in my case, the benefits far outweigh any potential problems. The hot flashes are gone; the mood swings much improved. (Oddly, I still feel my monthly cycles, even though they now come and go invisibly.) The HRT and anti-depressant are costly, but I do get to offset the expense: Natalie gave up diapers at about the same time I gave up tampons. We pass them by in the drug store with glee.

A missing child (and a cat)

I AM NOT SURE how to write a story with a missing protagonist and an indefinite conclusion, with false climaxes and a paucity of humor or irony to leaven the pages.

The narrative to date goes like this: we are adopting a child (announced last spring); we are trying to adopt a child (amended late fall); we lost a chance with a child (the holiday season's discouraging rewrite); we may not be successful at all (January's chill).

The core cast of characters includes my husband and I; our two daughters, Sera, now four, and Natalie, now three; and Anna, the caseworker assigned to our family from Hong Kong's adoption unit. Anna knows the most about this story, but, as is required of her by the Social Welfare Department, maintains a professional evasiveness about the outcome. I think she'd like to be more definitive (if only to put a stop to my phone calls), but, so far, she's resisted.

The story of the cat is much easier: we want a kitten, and we will get a kitten. The cat is a straightforward, unsubtle substitute for the child, and I offer no apologies for that. I want a guarantee, and this is the only one I can get.

The cat
Grace called this morning while I was at the dentist having a filling replaced. She left a carefully enunciated message, as if she were unaccustomed to answering machines, asking me to call her, she might have a kitten for us. She had gotten my name and number from the local veterinary clinic where the receptionist keeps two lists in a small black notebook, one filled with descriptions of animals needing new homes, and another, much shorter, list of

people interested in adopting a new pet. (This is the reverse, incidentally, of the lists Anna and her colleagues keep.)

I had given the receptionist a brief set of requirements: I was looking for a healthy, female, domestic shorthaired kitten. It was nice to make these few choices and have them go unchallenged. No mention was made of older cats, one-legged cats, tomcats, or extra-furry cats. No warnings about long waiting lists, no qualifications about what "healthy" might mean, no digging around in our personal lives to judge our suitability as an adoptive family, no paperwork, marriage certificate, birth certificates, proof of age, education, or income required. The receptionist made a few notes and said that she knew of a litter of kittens just born — they would be ready for homes in about six to eight weeks, shortly after the Christmas holidays.

It was the end of week seven when Grace called. From what I understood on the phone, Grace spends most of her free time rescuing stray animals. She checks in regularly with the vet's office, looking for leads on potential homes for her menagerie, then does her best to make a match. She currently had two kittens in foster care, she told me, would I be interested? (Finding foster care for animals is, according to Grace, just as difficult and nearly as important as finding foster care for children. I let it go.) A friend of hers was bringing the kittens over on the one-thirty ferry from the neighboring town of Mui Wo. I could give only the briefest response — the right half of my upper lip was still numb from a shot of Novocain — but we were able to arrange a meeting in the town plaza at two o'clock. Sera and Natalie knew a surprise was in the offing. Sera thought it might be a new umbrella. Natalie guessed a box of raisins. After some negotiation, they agreed that it would be a parrot.

The missing child

Twice a month, Anna and her colleagues meet with their supervisor in a conference room to match the available children with adoptive parents. Twice a month, I call Anna. Twice a month, she tells me that we were not matched with a child. Twice a month, she reassures me that she'll call me promptly if there is good news. Twice a month is too often to feel such loss.

Bill and I had put loss of this type behind us, or so I thought, when I accepted that I could no longer conceive a biological child. We had talked briefly about adoption some years ago; we reprised the idea when we learned that Hong Kong was laced with a comparatively efficient, caring, well-supported network of orphanages and foster homes for children who had been abandoned, orphaned, or otherwise legally separated from their birth parents. We started looking more closely at the families around us and started paying more attention to local adoption stories. A surprising number of the children that I had assumed were adopted from China into Western families were instead adopted from Hong Kong. Bill and I now consider Hong Kong home; it made sense to us to adopt locally. I made a visit to the Department of Welfare, and, during the course of an impromptu intake interview, learned that we met the basic requirements. We were invited to attend a briefing session for prospective parents. I was giddy with excitement.

The meeting was held in April in the Wan Chai offices of the Department of Welfare. (Actually, two meetings were held concurrently on separate floors: one was conducted in Cantonese for the local Chinese families, the other, in English for the Western families. Knowing what I now know about the policies and practices of the department, I can't help but wonder what was said to the local families.)

Bill and I were among the first of our group to arrive. We settled ourselves in two of the folding chairs arranged around a conference table and watched the others file in. One couple brought their nanny and their severely handicapped toddler; another couple brought their six-year-old daughter. We greeted each other with muted voices, as if we were meeting for the first time in a hospital waiting room.

The adoption unit assigned two caseworkers to lead the meeting — both young women, polished and professional, and both, as it soon became evident, adept at handling a roomful of anxious foreigners wanting answers and kids. The caseworkers loaded the table with boxes of cookies, candies, soft drinks, and sweetened green tea in bottles, and then began passing around a thick stack of handouts. We all scrambled around in our bags for pencils and pens and started making notes. Bill and I got the giggles.

Most of the information we received that day was basic, some of the information was surprising, and the most crucial information — the stuff of heartbreak — was carefully avoided. The first step, we were told, was to gather reams of documents, including our passports and visas, work permits, high school diplomas, college transcripts, birth and marriage certificates, medical records, income tax returns, three letters of reference, and a letter of support from our employers. We would also need to schedule comprehensive physical exams, including a chest X-rays to ferret out tuberculosis, which, as one would expect, carried a separate burden of paperwork. Finally, we were told to prepare ourselves for a home study to determine our suitability as prospective parents. One of the handouts was a timeline, and it looked like this part of the adoption process would take about six months.

Bill and I had already started gathering the required certificates and transcripts. We'd make an appointment with our family doctor for the following week, and we were as prepared as we could be for the home study. We were ready to move on; we wanted to talk about the children — one of them our new son or daughter.

Most likely a son, we soon learned. It was an odd moment: one of the caseworkers looked around the room and asked how many of us wanted to adopt a girl. The couple with the six-year-old raised their hands. A few others hesitated, wondering, I think, if the question was as casual as it sounded. Before they could decide, the caseworker shook her head at the hands in the air and told us that the demand among the local Chinese families was for baby girls by a ratio of nine to one. Consequently, the wait would be much longer if we wanted a girl. We glanced around the table at each other, confused. We were all piercingly aware of the tens of thousands of infant girls abandoned each month just across the border in mainland China. How could this powerful prejudice be turned on its head in neighboring Hong Kong?

As we began to sort through the implications of what we had been told, two things became clear: the caseworkers had ample statistics to back up their assertion — the preference for girls among local prospective parents was overwhelming — and, when pressed to explain the phenomenon, the caseworkers had little to offer. They shrugged apologetically and suggested that perhaps adoptive parents believe that girls will be more loving than boys. (I have since heard another explanation. A woman who has worked with orphaned and

abandoned children in Hong Kong for decades believes that the
phenomena has less to do with a fondness for girls than it does
with the legal and social status of adopted boys. Tradition favors
biological sons over adopted sons: it is a matter of bloodline and
inheritance rights.) Whatever the reason for this inverted preference, the awful irony is that Hong Kong's Chinese residents face
virtually insurmountable hurdles in adopting the abandoned
mainland girls. Despite the fact that Hong Kong is now a "special
administrative region" of China, local officials strictly, and some
say punitively, limit immigration from the mainland. China will
reluctantly allow a few of the adopted children to slip across the
border, but Hong Kong will not allow them to remain.

The caseworkers brought us back to solid ground before the
meeting broke up with a quick summary of the costs and legalities
of adopting in Hong Kong. We jotted down a few more notes,
then stood in line to get a copy of the initial, abbreviated application form. Not wanting to waste even a day of two, we filled it
out before we left the room and started kicking around a few
favorite boys' names on the way home.

We were wildly premature.

Three kids, one cat
Our plan to adopt a third child has met with some reservations
among our friends and acquaintances. I can understand their
response — adoption is a topic that raises a number of potentially
awkward questions. Do I have a fertility problem? Are Sera and
Natalie adopted? Will we be able to love an adopted child in the
same way and to the same degree that we love our biological
children? What if the child doesn't love us in return? Why take
on the burden of an interracial family? I don't much mind these
questions, even when they are motivated by base curiosity. I have
learned when to brush them off, when give the short answer, and
when to delve into a meatier discussion.

The question I do mind is the one for which I have no good
answer: Why another child? There is something about a third
child that, for many, tips a secret scale. I'm not sure why three.
Few seem to think that there is anything peculiar about wanting
one or two children, nor am I sure what the scale is measuring.

Our time and energy? Our financial reserves? Our family dynamics? Children come with no guarantees, but Bill and I have roughly the same level of confidence with bringing a third into our family as we did with the first and second (with all that might imply). That ought to be enough — it is, after all, a matter of the heart — but it doesn't seem to satisfy.

I feel this all the more acutely since the child will be adopted. I may be reading more into others' reaction than they intend, but I sense that what is being left unsaid is, "why take the risk?" as if an adopted child, with all of the mysteries and problems of his past, will somehow contaminate our family. It's like a double-whammy: a third child and adopted, at that. My instincts are aroused. I want to close my arms around my future son and ward off the scarring doubts hovering nearby.

Adopting a cat is clean. Nothing complicated, nothing risky. We will name her Lucy. She will cuddle up with me on those nights that Bill stays in China and keep me company during the day while I work at my computer. She and I will be companions, best buddies. She will not mind, I don't think, that initially she'll be catching the overflow of love that I cannot yet give a son.

A most unusual pregnancy
The six months following the initial adoption briefing were full of tasks assigned and tasks completed, each one moving the process forward in a quantifiable, satisfying progression. We filled out a sixteen-page application form, rounded up the testimonials from friends and employers, and completed our home study.

Before formally adding us to the waiting list, Anna, our caseworker, sat us down in our living room and laid out the official version of our strengths and "limitations" as prospective parents. Our strength, she said, was that we were obviously a loving, caring family. She did not list another. Our limitations were more numerous: we were Westerners; we already have two children and therefore could not provide an adopted child with our undivided attention; and Bill worked in China and, consequently, would not be as available to a new child as would a typical Hong Kong father.

We did not argue the first two points. We understood going in that the Department of Social Welfare first attempts to place their wards with local Chinese families. And there is no changing a departmental policy that favors single-child families, no matter how misguided I believe it to be. The last point was absurd. We added up the hours that Bill spent at home and asked Anna to compare that to a typical, grueling sixty- to eighty-hour Hong Kong workweek. We won the argument hands down, or so we thought. Anna agreed with our calculations, but, rather than dropping the limitation, she rewrote it. Now it counts against us that in case of an emergency Bill could potentially be unavailable for the three plus hours that it takes him to travel home from China. That shut us up.

Finally, before wrapping up her visit, Anna asked us to run through one more exercise. She wanted to talk in further detail about the type of child we would be willing to adopt. We had already supplied this information in our application, but Anna wanted to go through our choices one by one.

It started off simply. We had indicated that we were willing to adopt either a boy or girl, of any race or nationality, and we had asked to be matched with a baby under a year old. Anna nodded as we confirmed those first few choices and then moved down the list to the more complicated issues, all of which had to do with the child's health. Some of the questions were quite specific. Would we, for example, accept a child who had health problems with an unknown prognosis, such hepatitis B or a heart murmur? We had checked "yes." Anna pressed us, wanting to be sure that we understood the implications. Did we know that hepatitis B could increase the child's risk of liver cancer in later life? Did we know that a heart murmur could be indicative of a serious medical condition? We did. Our conversation followed the same pattern through a maze of health problems ranging from asthma to cleft palates. Anna glanced up as she read through the list to make sure that we were still nodding. We were.

Next we came to the questions that had caused Bill and I to equivocate — the ones that seemed designed to either eliminate or include impossibly broad categories of children in a single stroke. We had answered these with a "maybe," as is allowed for on the application form. The idea, as we understood it, was that we could make a decision once we had more information to go on. Anna conceded that "maybe" was a legitimate option, but she preferred a straightforward yes or no. We focused first on item *f:* "Will both of you accept a child from parents with a history of drug addiction?" "It depends," was the best that we could do. Would we accept a child whose mother had shot up heroin for the duration of her pregnancy? Probably not. Would we accept a child whose mother had occasionally used milder drugs? Probably so. Anna wanted more. "Which drugs, and on how many occasions?" she asked. Bill and I conferred, trying, without much success, to come up with a more precise answer. We had asked our family doctor about prenatal drug use, and she had told us that it would be almost impossible to make an informed decision without knowing more than just the name of the drug. The same was true for a sub-heading of *f:* "Will both of you accept a child with psychiatric problems in parents or parents' extended family?" We were wary about taking on a child whose parents suffered from serious mental illness, but we were much less concerned about problems in his extended family. And, of course, we would want to know the specific nature of the mental illness. The more we talked, the more we felt the subtlety of the questions, and the more difficult it became to carve out neat answers. The conversation felt as if it were tracking backwards.

If Anna was frustrated, she did not let it show, even though we were uncomfortably aware that we weren't making her job any easier. She had previously explained to us that the caseworkers typically have only one day to study the files of the children newly freed for adoption before they meet for the matching panel. As it is, they spend many frantic hours on the phone with prospective parents reciting the details of a child's history and trying to get a clear commitment before the meeting convenes the next day. Applications swamped with "maybe"s mean more hesitations, consultations, and delays than the system can afford. Bill and I were sympathetic, but only to a point. The more we restricted our choices, the more we risked ruling out a child who, had we known more about him, could have become a part of our family. Efficiency was not a fair trade for a child. We stuck to our "maybe"s.

As hard as that was, it was not as painful as our rapid progression through the questions to which we had answered "no." We would not take a child with severe physical or mental handicaps. Nor would we take a child with significant developmental or behavioral problems. Anna did not ask us to justify our choices, but I tried nevertheless: we did not have the resources — time, energy, money, know-how — to take on a physically or mentally handicapped child, nor would it be fair to Sera and Natalie. What I said is true, as far as it goes, but it feels like window-dressing. The deeper truth, the more honest truth, is that I am frightened of the commitment, frightened of turning over too much of my life to a child whose needs could overwhelm me. In this, Bill and I are in the clear majority. Few are willing or able to take on these children. The healthy babies are snapped up; the others linger on, some in foster care, some in institutions that will eventually become the only home they know. Each "no" splattered me with shame.

Anna left us with a promise to let us know when we were placed on the waiting list — a week or two, at most. My third pregnancy was beginning to unfold.

September

I sneak quick glances at the pregnant women I see on the streets of Hong Kong. *Is that my baby?* Or, perhaps our baby has already been born, and is now lying in a crib at an orphanage waiting for us. Does anyone pick him up when he cries in the middle of the night? *Hold on,* I want to tell him. *Be strong. We're coming.* I feel the first growth of the same fierce bonding instincts that overtook me during my two biological pregnancies, but this time the shoots and tendrils have nothing to grasp onto. Exposed and vulnerable, they search for their intended target.

I call Anna for the second time since we were added to the waiting list at the beginning of the month. September's matching panels have brought us no news. Anna is good-humored about my calls and teases me about being impatient. Later that day, I buy another book on raising adopted children. It is the only shopping that I have allowed myself to do for the new baby.

October passes much like September. By the end of November, my phone conversations with Anna have taken on a one-way edge. What I want from her (other than a child) is information. What more can she tell me about the wait? I try to coax her into offering an estimate, a best guess. It all depends, Anna says. It could be tomorrow, if the right child comes along. I know that, I respond. But how far out in time should I extend the other end of the parenthesis? She tries phrasing her answer differently, packaging a shrug inside elastic words that give away nothing. I bite my tongue. I like Anna, I believe she likes us, and I do not want to risk marring the relationship. If I push her too hard, I might earn a black mark for being overly aggressive (surely a bad trait in a parent) or culturally insensitive to the Chinese way of doing things. Anna, more than ten years my junior, has been unfailingly pleasant with me, but I am acutely aware of the non-negotiable power that she wields over the future of my family. One might growl and snarl at the recalcitrant bureaucrat behind the counter of, say, the Department of Motor Vehicles without risking much in the way of retribution, but self-presentation is everything in the adoption game. Like all adoptive parents, I will have to learn to manage a pregnancy that has no due date.

The only thing we can be certain of is that when our son does come, he will be a "special needs" child, despite the restrictions we checked off on our application form. The classification was originally intended to identify children with significant physical or mental handicaps, but has instead turned into a catchall, a trap, that ensnares children who are simply less than perfect or who have passed what Anna calls "that tender age." It nets children with birthmarks (considered by many Chinese to bring bad luck); children, especially boys, who are older than three or four; children with complicated family backgrounds; even children born with entirely treatable and, in many cases, minor medical conditions. The classification is chilling in its inclusiveness, since, more often than not, it means that the children will have a great deal of difficulty finding homes. Sera, born with birthmarks on her hip and thigh, would have had difficulty being placed in an adoptive home. My sister, born with a crossed eye, would have had the same trouble, as would have my brother, born with a spectacular case of jaundice.

The drive for perfection among local adoptive parents is so intense that a few years ago the Department of Social Welfare stopped allowing parents to meet the child they had been matched with until the parents had made a firm commitment to the adoption. The caseworkers were tired of, and sickened by, the window-shopping that had become commonplace at the orphanages. Infants were rejected because their eyes were too slanted, or because their skin was too dark, or because their hair was growing "funny." The new rule has mitigated, but not eliminated, the problem. There is nothing that can be done about those who pile up the "no" answers on the application form until it is virtually impossible for any but a seemingly flawless child to squeeze through. (One wonders what happens to these families as the real child emerges from behind the illusion of perfection.) As a last resort, special needs children are placed abroad, often with American families, who, for what-ever reason, are more open to these children than are Hong Kong natives.

From everything that Bill and I had been told, these special needs children are in desperate need of homes. It seemed reason-able, then, for us to expect to be matched with a child sooner rather than later. We prepared ourselves for a relatively quick placement, but, because Anna was right, and I am impatient, I mentally added six months to the process, just to keep my expectations on the safe side.

As the months ticked by, my optimism began to fade.

December
Anna called to invite us to a Christmas party hosted by the Department of Social Welfare. The invitees were the special needs children awaiting placement and any prospective parents the caseworkers could rope in. We were easy. I responded with the bright, brittle, over-eagerness of a sixteen-year-old girl who does not get asked out on many dates.

The party was set for noon on December 15th. Anna asked us to bring Sera and Natalie along. We would all have lunch, play games, hand around holiday treats, and then — well, and then what? Suddenly, the enormity of what we were doing took hold. The holiday celebration was, of course, little more than a pretense, something to tell the kids to gloss over the cruelty of being set out on display. Even assuming all of the adults came with only the best of intentions and comported themselves with discretion, the older children and, perhaps, some of the younger ones as well, would know they were being assessed. We were going, I was sure of that, but I also knew that I'd walk into the party discomforted by the weight of my conscience trailing behind me like an uninvited and unacknowledged guest. The only argument strong enough to balance the surety of inflicting pain was that some of the children might find a home. Anna fed us success stories from past parties: a couple who wanted an infant instead adopted six-year-old twins; another couple, also waiting for a baby, attended reluctantly, fell for a five-year-old girl eating a hot dog and made the commitment to adopt her that same afternoon.

The doors to the restaurant were still locked when we arrived. It was a beautiful day, so we walked the short distance to the harbor and watched the Star ferry make the ten-minute crossing from Kowloon to Central. When we returned, the doors were propped open, and Sera and Natalie ran in ahead of Bill and me. Inside was a surge of activity. The waiters and waitresses were finishing setting up the buffet line, and the representatives from the department were transferring clipboards and notepads from boxes stacked knee-high on the floor to the registration table. I checked my watch — a nervous tick — it was ten minutes past noon. I occupied myself with chasing down Sera and Natalie, who were trying to unwrap the bags of trinkets placed in the center of each table, while Bill stood uncertainly in front of the registration table looking for Anna. We were both surprised to see that no games or play areas had been set up for the children.

Bill joined us a few minutes later with our table assignment and nametags, which we obediently stuck to our chests. It was not until after the party was over that I learned that the small stickers on the children's tags — either a yellow butterfly or a purple frog — were meant to indicate which children were available for adoption and which were not.

While the other guests trickled in, Bill and I tried to figure out the etiquette of the event. The narrow, crowded room and formal seating arrangements discouraged mingling, and the delicacy of the event stifled the ice-breaking small talk that would, under more normal circumstances, begin with the children and ripple outward to engage the adults. Bill and I exchanged awkward greetings with the others seated at our table. A Chinese couple sat next to Bill; a quiet little boy and the equally quiet adult with him sat next to me; and at the end of the table, a toddler and a woman Anna later introduced as the girl's foster mother filled out our group of ten.

After twenty minutes of shifting around in our chairs and taking guesses at what we were supposed to be doing with ourselves, one of the event coordinators announced that the buffet lunch was ready and invited us to join the slow shuffle toward the front of the restaurant. The jostling about gave me an opportunity to take Anna aside and whisper a question about the two children sitting at our table. Were the seating arrangements deliberate? Mm, she answered, noncommittally. With a tilt of her head at the little girl still seated at the end of our table, Anna told me that her name was Man-Yee, that she was two years old, and that she was available for adoption. Wai Ming, the shy boy sitting next to me, was five, and he, too, would be available for adoption within the next few months. Anna had apparently noticed me trying to make him laugh. Back at our seats, while the children lowered their heads in concentration over the noodles, lunchmeats, and wiggling piles of colored jello on their plates, I passed the information to Bill. He shot me a warning glance. Adopting Wai Ming, Bill was signaling, was out of the question.

It was the first move in what would become a month-long dance of dissension between us. Anna had been urging us for some time to consider adopting an older child, and it had been fairly easy to convince us to stretch our preferences to include two- and three-year-olds. But Bill drew the line at three. A four-year-old, he feared, might disrupt the dynamics between Sera and Natalie, and a child older than four would knock Sera from her oldest-child-in-the-family throne. I was less sure about the importance of birth order, but I did have concerns about adopting a child who had spent five or six years bouncing around between orphanages and foster homes. Birth to age three seemed like a fair compromise.

I had no business, then, falling for Wai Ming, and he had no business falling for Bill. If I spent a good deal of the party surreptitiously watching Wai Ming, he spent it doing the same with Bill. I would catch him stealing glances across the table, studying Bill with an intensity that fascinated me. He watched him eat, he watched him help Natalie with her lunch, he watched him as he escorted our kids back to the buffet table for seconds. It was only when Bill was absent from the immediate scene that I was able to tease Wai Ming (in pantomime) about the embroidered frog jumping up the back of his shirt, or about the jello that kept slipping from his fork.

Bill noticed what was happening, and it made him uncomfortable — *set up,* was how he put it to me later that afternoon. He tried re-directing my attention to Man-Yee, who, by the end of the party, was being passed around the room from one adoring adult to another. She was a lovely, delicate child, and no one seemed troubled by the angry-looking birthmark on her lower right eyelid. But would the same families be willing to adopt her? Would we stand a chance? There was no telling. I said nothing further about Wai Ming, but I did make a note of his name on a paper napkin, which I then tucked away in my wallet. On the way out the door, we caught up with Anna, and this time, Bill asked most of the questions.

He started with procedure: *What's our next move?* The question had to be asked — we had no idea how we were supposed to indicate our interest in the children we had just met — but it felt uncomfortably like bidding on a new house in a tight real-estate market. Anna's answer, essentially, was *wait.* The next matching panel, she said, would be held at the beginning of January. Prior to that, the case-workers would have to sort out the feedback they had received from the prospective parents at the party — many people might express interest in the same child. Anna was leaving the next morning for a two-week vacation, but when she got back she would pull the file on Man-Yee and give us more information about her. She might as well have said two years. Waiting two more weeks, after being so close to a room full of adoptable children, seemed unbearable.

Bill, who, until this point, had been much more patient with the process than I, must have felt the same: he would not take no for an answer. After some back-and-forth, Anna relented, and told us to call the department's in-take worker on the following Monday. Anna would leave word with her colleague to release the information to us. Bill and I walked back to the ferry musing over the strangeness of meeting one's future child at a Christmas party. "Maybe," I said. "Maybe," he replied.

Man-Yee was born in April of 1999 to a single mother and an unknown father. Her mother, herself a victim of a broken, unstable home, was shunted around in childhood from relative to relative, suffered from mild psychiatric problems, and proved incapable of caring for Man-Yee. Man-Yee was placed in a foster home shortly after her first birthday. She had a few minor health problems at birth, but had recently earned a clean bill of health, and, according to her foster mother, had adjusted well to her temporary home.

I asked the in-take worker to look up Wai Ming's file. "Sure," she said, and put me on hold. Wai Ming, she told me when she returned, came from a very troubled background. His mother was fifteen years old when she became pregnant. She did not know who fathered the child. She had used marijuana and tranquilizers "several times" during her pregnancy. She had spent time in prison; she had neglected and physically abused Wai Ming, as had her boyfriends. He had been placed in foster care when he was three. The in-take worker recited from the notes in his file: his health was good, he liked to hike, he had some difficulty with speech articulation, he was angry at his mother, he displayed cheerful, appropriate behavior at school and with his foster mother. Because he had been an abused child, because his mother had used drugs during her pregnancy, and because he was five, going on six, he would be very difficult to place in a permanent home. Before I hung up, the in-take worker added that Wai Ming had been assigned to our table at the party because he had asked to meet an American.

That evening after Bill returned home from work, we took a long meandering walk through our neighborhood, and I recited what I had learned, beginning with Man-Yee. Everything sounded perfect, we both agreed. We'd take her into our home in a heartbeat. Three daughters — it was what we had originally imagined when we began the adoption process; it still felt right.

Next, I tentatively broached the subject of Wai Ming. Bill was willing to listen, but warned me straight off that he still felt strongly about the negative consequences of adopting a child older than Sera. I stumbled around, trying to find the right words to describe the depth of my feelings for the boy. How to make the improbable sound plausible? In truth, I knew even then that I would go to the end of the earth for him, but I also knew that saying so to Bill would only serve to make him defensive. We found a temporary solution in my passion for research. I would look up everything I could find on birth-order and adoption. I would talk to child-development experts and other parents with both biological and adopted children. I would poll friends and family, collecting gut reactions from people I love and trust. I had two goals: the first, to gather solid information; the second, to buy time while Bill had a chance to think things over and form a picture in his mind of a different family dynamic.

We flew to Seattle to spend Christmas with my family. Anna would return to work on Monday, January 1st; the next matching panel would be held two days later. I calculated the time difference — at that time of year, Seattle is sixteen hours behind Hong Kong. I gave Anna two hours to get her workday underway and called her from the back bedroom of my parents' house at 6:00 PM West Coast time, 10:00 AM Hong Kong time.

We exchanged brief reports of holidays well spent, then, using the excuse of expensive long-distance phone rates, I jumped in: could we adopt Man-Yee? And what about Wai Ming? "Wai Ming?" she responded, sounding surprised. "But he's five." I summarized for her the conversations Bill and I had had since the party. When I had finished, we backed up to discuss Man-Yee. Her case, Anna said, would be going before the matching panel on Wednesday. Having just returned to the office, she was not sure if anyone else had expressed interest in Man-Yee, but she thought it likely. She would not hazard a guess about our chances of success. Instead, she reiterated what she had said to me before: as harsh as it sounded, she and her colleagues were advocates for the children, not the waiting parents. The placements were based on the child's best interest. "Yes, I understand. That's as it should be," I replied truthfully and stopped myself from saying more. I could only ask that our names be shuffled around with the rest when Man-Yee's future was being decided.

Anna turned the conversation back to Wai Ming, who was one of the children on her caseload. It seemed she, too, had a soft spot for him, describing him as a quiet, delightful, well-adjusted boy, despite his difficult early years. The paperwork required to free him for adoption, though, would not be complete for another month or two, and until that was wrapped up, he would remain in foster care. Anna sounded genuinely glad to hear of our interest and asked me to let her know what my research turned up. I promised, and we made an appointment to speak again after Wednesday's matching panel. I hung up the phone, poured myself a glass of wine, and reported the details of the conversation to my family. We spent the rest of the evening working out the possible scenarios. My favorite: adopt both children.

It was eleven o'clock on Tuesday evening when I called Anna — late Wednesday afternoon in Hong Kong. She got right to the point: Man-Yee had been placed with another family. "I'm sorry," she said. "Are you very disappointed?" I shouldn't have been. I should have known to expect it when Anna told me that other families — Chinese families — had expressed interest in Man-Yee. But I was disappointed, horribly so. This must be what it feels like to experience a false pregnancy, I thought to myself. I hoped Anna couldn't hear me crying.

"Are we ever going to get a child?" I blurted out. I imagined our file being shuffled to the bottom of the stack each time a child became available. Maybe there was a problem that Anna hadn't had the heart to tell us about. Or had she seen through us during the home study? Had she sensed that we were less than forthright with her about our character flaws and our shortcomings as parents, as humans? Anna listened while I poured out these desperate questions. My distress must have shot across the six thousand miles of telephone cable at full strength, as, by way of an answer, she offered me a consolation prize: information.

What I learned was crushing (which may be why the information is withheld from prospective parents). At any given time, there are at least sixty to seventy families on the waiting list, Anna told me, with more being added every month. Those families are competing for a dwindling number of infants — sometimes, as few as three or four children per matching panel. And because of our so-called limitations, nearly all of the other families had priority over us.

"But what about the special needs children?" I asked.

"You met them all at the party," Anna replied. I was stunned. That meant that with the exception of Man-Yee, there was not a single special needs child currently available for adoption that fell within the boundaries of our stated preferences. I was beginning to understand the odds; it felt like eating lead.

What I still did not understand was why some of my acquaintances had, as recently as a year or two ago, been matched with a child within a six- to eight-month period, tops. "Things have changed in the last few years," Anna said.

"Like what?" I asked.

"Well, more and more girls are traveling to Shenzhen for abortions," she replied.

I remembered an article I had recently read in the newspaper about promiscuity among Hong Kong's youth. A young man bragged to the reporter that he planned to have sex with his girlfriend during the upcoming Chinese New Year holiday. He wasn't worried about safe sex; he had set aside enough money to pay for an abortion if his girlfriend became pregnant. (The other dangers of unprotected sex apparently did not worry him, or had not occurred to him.) I could see where Anna was going: abortions are legal in Hong Kong, but they are not cheap, nor are they conducted under a cloak of anonymity, and this had, in the past, discouraged many young women from aborting unwanted pregnancies. A spate of newly established abortion clinics (some legitimate, some shady) in Shenzhen, a populous, modern Chinese city just half-an-hour away by train, have dramatically changed the picture. There, abortions are cheap and easy to obtain, particularly if one is willing to chance a botched operation. Many are.

I realized I had been pestering Anna with the wrong question: I shouldn't have been asking *when* we would get a child, but *if* we would get a child. She would not, perhaps could not, give me a direct answer, but I was learning how to read between the lines of our conversations. Our chances were not good.

Lucy
We arrived in the plaza fifteen minutes early and sat down at one of the outdoor picnic tables to wait for Grace. Sera and Natalie were

jumping around in excitement, although they still had no idea what shape the promised surprise would take. Bill wandered off to buy a coke. I was anxious, worried that Grace might have already given the kitten to someone else. Shortly after the ferry from Mui Wo docked, I spotted a young Chinese woman walking toward the plaza with a rambunctious puppy dancing around her heels. She was dressed in tight-fitting black jeans, high-heeled boots, and a long-sleeved lime-green sweater with matching faux-fir trim at the collar and cuffs. A more disheveled looking man followed close behind her, lugging a portable dog kennel with one hand and a cat carrier with the other. It had to be Grace and her friend; I waved them down.

The puppy provided us with a few minutes of cover. Sera and Natalie immediately dropped down on their hands and knees to chase him around under the picnic table, while I checked with Grace to make sure that it was our kitten in the cat carrier and that it was available for us to take home that afternoon as planned. "Yes, yes," she said, nodding vigorously. As if on cue, her friend, Tom, turned his attention from the puppy to the cat carrier, and I convinced Sera and Natalie to do the same.

"This is our surprise," I told them. "We have a new kitten. Her name is Lucy." Natalie looked up at me and let out a soft squeal. Sera was all business, conducting a close inspection of the wire-mesh door on the cat carrier and trying to figure out how to spring it. "Oh, there are two in there!" she announced. I leaned in for a closer look and saw two black and tan tiger-stripped kittens fitted together like pieces of a puzzle. One of them lifted its head, peered back at me, and, apparently not much interested in what it saw, rose for a lazy, arched stretch. After a quick sniff or two at the unfamiliar surroundings, the cat nudged its way back into place against its still-sleeping littermate.

Sera whipped her head around and demanded of the adults, "Which one is Lucy?"

"I don't know," I told her. Grace and Bill had stepped back from the table, leaving Tom and I to work out the details of the transfer. "Are they both girls?" I asked him.

"No," he answered. "There's one boy and one girl."

"Which is which?"

Tom lifted one of the kittens out of the carrier and took a close look at its back-end. "This is the boy, I'm pretty sure. Let me check the other one," he said, swapping the kittens. He was surer of his second inspection. "This is the girl," he said firmly. Before I could say anything, he put her back in the carrier with her brother. I looked over at him, surprised. I was about to ask if I could transfer Lucy into our carrier before I confused her with her brother, but Tom had pulled out a small packet of pills and wanted to tell me about the medication. It was for a bacterial infection common to stray cats, he said, and the kittens would need to finish the seven days worth of remaining antibiotics. "So we need to split them up, right?" I asked. Now Tom looked surprised.

"Both kittens are on the antibiotics," he answered.

"Yeah, but I only need Lucy's half."

"You're only taking one cat?" he asked, with what I thought was exaggerated incredulity.

"Yes," I said, glancing over at Grace. In a move that could not have been better choreographed, both she and Bill retreated a further two steps away from the table. "Yes," I said again, more firmly, "the female. Lucy. That's what I told Grace on the phone."

"But these two can't be split up. They're really close."

I looked again at Grace, trying to draw her into the conversation as an ally, but she refused to meet my eye. Tom was shaking his head, preparing to further his argument. "Look," I said, cutting him off, "we can only take one cat. That's the deal I made with Grace. It's not fair to back out of it now." I could hear my voice rising with the first flush of anger. With a conciliatory gesture and the tone of voice a parent would take with a precocious child demanding a pet elephant, Tom explained to me that having two cats is always better than having one — they are happier with cat companionship than with human companionship. "Maybe," I said, "but I don't want two cats. Grace agreed to give us Lucy," I added stubbornly. I realized I was glaring at Tom.

"Why don't I call the guy who has been taking care of the litter," he offered, pulling out his mobile phone. "If he thinks it's alright to separate the kittens, I will. Okay?"

"Okay," I replied, and concentrated on relaxing my tensed shoulders. Stupid to get so worked up, I thought, but I should have seen it coming. The excess of emotion now riding so close to the surface was left over from a volatile discussion Bill and I had had about Wai Ming a few days earlier. Anna had set it off with a phone call shortly after we returned to Hong Kong from Seattle, wanting to know if we were still interested in pursuing his adoption. I told her the truth: I hadn't yet summoned the courage to reopen the conversation with Bill. The holiday's upset was too fresh and I was afraid Bill might draw blood (albeit unintentionally) if he had decided against adopting an older child in general, and Wai Ming in particular. Anna's call gave me the push I needed.

We talked it over sitting on the verandah of a small, open-air bar overlooking a stretch of rocky beach in one of the neighboring fishing villages. It was an unusually warm afternoon, and the waterfront was crowded with kids, a handful of scraggly-looking dogs, and villagers wading into the water with fishing poles and buckets. We listened to the sounds of Cantonese ricocheting off the rocks as our own conversation lurched about in fits and starts: both of us were nervous about slamming straightaway into a dead end. I rolled my coaster back and forth across the sticky surface of the table as I explained to Bill that we were on our own with the decision. I had done my research, which proved to be simple since there is very little written about adoption and birth order, and our family and friends had been smart enough to tell me that they would support our decision no matter which way it swung.

"Convince me," Bill said. "I'm willing to be talked into this."

"Bad idea," I replied, though the temptation was great. "Imagine how much you could grow to resent me if I talked you into an adoption that you really weren't sure about."

"Yeah, maybe," he said.

"Let me try doing this as straight as I can." I did my best to keep my emotions in check as I laid out my arguments. Bill listened carefully, but I had nothing new to offer. I had fallen in love with Wai Ming over a plate of jello. I badly wanted him to be my son. *It was meant to be,* I said more than once.

It was Bill's turn. His argument was as brief and stale as mine: Sera deserves to keep her place as the oldest child in our family.

We took more than an hour shaping our one-note arguments into as many different forms as we could invent, then, defeated, finished our beer and hiked the two miles back to our apartment in silence. We would try again in a week or two. I wasn't willing to push Bill into this, but I also wasn't willing to let Wai Ming slip away by default.

Tom clicked off his phone and nodded his consent. We could take Lucy and he would find another home for her brother. "Ha!" I wanted to shout. We untangled the two kittens, transferred Lucy into our cat carrier, and hustled off to the vet's office for Lucy's first round of shots and a general check-up.

Yes

"Okay," Bill said. "Let's do it."

"Okay? Just like that?" I asked.

"Yeah, just like that. I told you that I just needed to know that Sera wouldn't be hurt by our decision. If Yvonne said we could make it work, then let's call Anna."

I blew a mental kiss to Yvonne, a child development expert our pediatrician had put me in touch with, and called Anna.

It was nearly six o'clock, but Anna was still in her office. "Anna," I shouted, "Guess what? We want to adopt Wai Ming!"

"Oh," she said, "that makes me very happy!"

"Me too," I answered.

"But what about Bill?" Anna asked. "Did he change his mind?"

"Yes, he did," I said, and filled her in on the details of my appointment with Yvonne earlier that day. I had put Bill's question to her as bluntly as I could: Was there any evidence to suggest that adopting an older child would be disruptive or harmful to Sera or Natalie? She answered cautiously. "Adopting a child, no matter what his or her age, will change the family dynamics, perhaps dramatically. You'll all need time to adjust." I explained Bill's specific fears about Sera. She nodded. "Yes," she said, "Sera will lose her position as the oldest child. But if you adopt a younger child, Natalie will lose her position as the baby." The key to making the adoption work, she continued, was to make sure that each child felt like they had an important role in the family. This made good sense to me, but I wanted to push it one step further, just to be sure. I told her everything I knew about Wai Ming and asked her if she had any reason to think that proceeding with the adoption was a bad idea. "No," she answered. "None at all." I danced out of her office and called Bill with my news.

"That's all it took," I told Anna.

"I'm very glad," Anna repeated, and for the first time in months, I felt like Anna, Bill, and I were all pulling in the same direction. Anna reminded me that Wai Ming's paperwork was not yet complete. "It should be finished by the end of February," she said.

"I can wait," I answered.

"And you have to remember that Wai Ming could be matched with another family," Anna added.

"Has anyone else expressed an interest in him?" I asked.

"Not to me," she answered, "but I'll have to check with the other caseworkers. It's better to wait until the paperwork is done." I decided to interpret her caution as pro forma.

"Okay, I'll hold off buying model airplanes and baseball caps," I tell her. "I don't want to jinx anything. But tell your colleagues to hurry up with that paperwork, okay?" Anna is laughing as we end the conversation.

The sleepover

Lucy lies next to my head, her paws loosely tangled in my hair, and purrs in my ear. She is a beautiful cat, tawny colored, with black stripes running down her back and swirling around her legs like melted chocolate. And like cats everywhere, she has taken over our household, doing what she likes when she likes, regardless of our rules. She loves to sit on Sera's lap, but has chosen to sleep at night with Natalie. She keeps me company during the day while I'm working at my computer, except for a few hours in the early afternoon — that time is reserved solely for our nanny, Yolly. Bill can count on her to sit with him on the sofa for a bit in the evening after the kids go to bed. The rest of her time she spends tearing around the apartment, transforming chairs into trampolines, curtains into climbing walls, polished wood floors into a skating rink. She stages elaborate, fierce battles with hair clips, rubber bands, crayons, loose screws — anything she can paw free from a drawer or countertop into formation on the field. When the skirmishes erupt at three o'clock in the morning, she is sent for a time-out in the guestroom.

Tonight, Lucy has joined Sera, Natalie, and me for her first sleepover. We do this on occasion, usually on Sunday evenings after Bill has left for China. The girls are most often the ones to initiate the pajama parties, throwing themselves pell-mell across our king-sized bed, but this time, it was my idea. I wanted to giggle with them under the covers, teasing Lucy with three sets of catch-me-if-you-can-toes. I wanted to watch them sleep, see their dreams flit across their bodies. I wanted to feel their arms flung across my chest, their legs kicking against mine. I sleep intermittently, nudged time and again out of a light sleep by the ever-shifting bodies. Natalie rolls over Sera and wedges herself against Lucy and me. Sera rotates out of the way and falls out of bed, landing on a pile of cushions stacked on the floor for that very purpose. Lucy jumps down to investigate. We stretch out, ball up, roll together, and gravitate toward the middle of the bed, as if to leave enough room for others to join us.

I have had one last conversation with Anna. Wai Ming's mother will not sign the last piece of paper required to free her son for adoption. She does not want him back — he is well and good abandoned — but she apparently has had enough of the Department of Social Welfare, along with the caseworkers and their documents. The blow will fall hard on Wai Ming. His case will have to go to court; it will take months to resolve. Something flutters shut in my chest, like the keys on a flute after the last note has been fingered. I will not withdraw our application, but neither will I call Anna again.

Lucy sighs and shifts position on my pillow. I pull Sera and Natalie close and coil my love tightly around my sleeping children.

Stop please

WE ARE IN A TAXI, Bill, Sera, Natalie and I, on our way home from a morning spent at the park. Natalie has learned to repeat a phrase that she hears only in taxis — *li do* — which means "right here" in Cantonese. We use it, obviously, to signal to the driver that we'd like him to stop "right here." As we near our apartment, Natalie sings out *"li do."* The taxi driver immediately slows down, looks over his shoulder at us, and repeats *"li do?"* "No," Bill says, "keep going." Half a minute later, Natalie tries again: *"li do,"* which occasions the same response from the driver. "No," Bill says in a louder voice, "keep going!" His temper is frayed from a long morning with the kids. I dare not ask, although I'd like to, if he is becoming exasperated with Natalie for issuing commands, or with the taxi driver for taking instruction from a three-year-old. We are close to home, but not yet there, and Natalie cannot resist. *"Li do!"* "Just stop!" Bill shouts at Natalie. The driver skids to a sudden stop, and we have no choice but to save face and pile out of the taxi, half a block from home.

Hick

IT IS TEN O'CLOCK in the morning, and the half-mile long series of one-way, linked escalators and moving sidewalks that climb a steep slope on Hong Kong Island (and, incidentally, comprises the world's longest outdoor escalator) is about to shut down. A man in a rumpled blue uniform and black cap takes his position obstructing the entrance to the uppermost set of mechanized steps, his face stern, walkie-talkie at the ready, arms and legs spread wide to prevent trouble-makers from dashing past him for a quick ride down the hill. His colleague, who cannot possibly top five feet, waits for the last person to clear the bottom step, then throws a body-block across the exit.

The escalators, which since early morning have been carrying commuters down the hillside from their residential neighborhood to their jobs in the financial district, will grind to a stop for ten or fifteen minutes, then reverse direction and run up-hill until late at night. The men in blue, whose job it is to execute this reversal, are as serious as police at a crime scene, moving slowly and cautiously down each link in the chain of escalators, barking orders into their walkie-talkies, fending off impatient passengers, and signaling to an invisible comrade, *throw the switch!* The sophisticated urbanites en route to their offices in one of the world's most expensive districts abandon the pretense of civility and begin jostling and elbowing each other to gain an advantaged position on the escalator, hoping to make it to the bottom before it is too late.

Under most circumstances I would stop to watch the scene, but on this occasion I am late for an appointment to have my hair cut, and I too find myself eyeing the escalator police and plotting ways to slip by them. I have a leg up over most of the crowd: I am wearing my tennis shoes, and I can easily out-maneuver the women in their chic high-heeled mules and even most of the men who would prefer not to chance scuffing their shoe leather. My tennis shoes serve me well on the escalator, but once I land in the financial district, a familiar sensation creeps up on me from around my ankles — I feel like a hick, and I blame my shoes.

Tennis shoes have not caught on in Hong Kong, and working women in particular seem to eschew the American habit of tucking one's high heels under the desk and throwing on a sensible pair of shoes to run errands at lunch time. To make matters worse, the styles this season favor slips of shoes held on by single strap or two. They come in a rainbow of colors, decorated with bangles, embroidery, sequins, feathers, and bits of fluff, and no one seems to think twice about wearing these baby-doll shoes around town. I lengthen my stride, throw my shoulders back, and move as purposely as I can past the designer boutiques, the international banking headquarters, the well-dressed, well-shod crowds, trying to convey a sense of fleet-footed purpose — all to justify my beat-up tennis shoes.

My confidence level does not improve much when I arrive at the hair salon. It is a ridiculously expensive place, and I am intimidated by both the staff and the clientele. There are countless other places in Hong Kong that offer less expensive hair cuts, but the chances of finding a stylist who speaks good English is spotty, and I'm not brave enough to communicate what I'm after through sign language. The young man, Cliff, who cuts my hair, speaks English and does a competent job, and for that I am willing to pay top dollar.

An employee, whose sole job seems to be to dress the clients, meets me at the door and wraps me in a purplish-brown gown. It is ugly, and I relax — the gowns are a great equalizer. Within a few seconds of sitting down, another employee, who also has a one-line job description, offers me tea, coffee, and sweets. Now comes the magnificent part of this hair cut: the massage. The stylists, including Cliff, have a bevy of male assistants who double as masseurs. (I note with interest that on this visit they are all wearing jeans with fringed, tie-dyed scarves knotted low around their hips.) Cliff's assistant, whose name I cannot pronounce, is tall, scrawny, and ungainly. His face is covered with acne, and I have a hard time imagining that he has cleared his teenage years.

But what he can do with his hands makes him a very important person in my life, and on each visit to the salon, I pray that he (let's call him Joe) has not found another job.

We start with the wash, and it is what a wash should be — thorough, cleansing, pleasant, relaxing — all good things. But once my hair is coated with a palm-full of conditioning goo, Joe begins the massage and the experience tops out at exquisite. He spends a long time working over every inch of my scalp, then, when I think it can't get any better, he takes on the knots in my neck and shoulders. My face is next. I'd never before had a face massage, and although I draw the line at having my eyeballs massaged, no matter how delicate the touch, it's remarkable what well-applied pressure can do for the stress lodged in my temples and jaw. Same goes for my hands — palms, fingers, and wrists get individual attention. Lastly, he cleans my ears; this I could do without.

I have entered something akin to a meditative trance by the time I get back to Cliff's styling chair and it's a good thing because I swear he cuts my hair one strand at a time. He has a habit of lifting a section of hair off my head, letting it drop, and studying the way it falls. After a moment of consideration, he will carefully cut a few pieces, and then repeat the process. Is this a sign of extreme care, or extreme incompetence? I'm not sure, but I do like the results, and I can be guaranteed of Cliff's full attention if, after he dries and styles my new do, I request minor alterations. No one, including myself, has ever demonstrated this much interest in my hair.

The whole affair takes over two hours, but I don't care. I feel like a million bucks, well-coifed and ready to step out among the glitterati. The receptionist nods her approval when I stop at the front desk to hand over Bill's paycheck. I glide back up the escalator with my dignity restored. My shoes may look goofy, but my neck and shoulders are loose, my head tingles, and my hair looks great.

Changes

THIS IS A DAY that requires uncommon courage, and I am not up to it. I would rather stay in bed, low to the ground, evading the changes that are waiting to touch down in my life.

My father is ill, and my sister, who is with him in Seattle, fears he might be dying. Her e-mail message was waiting for me when I got up this morning — worried, sad, hesitant about associating death with our father, as if the proximity of the words alone might be enough to touch off a dreaded chain of events involving his failing heart, failing kidneys, and failing spirit. My stepmother, Mary, who, out of a storied kind of love and single-minded determination, has kept him alive the past few years, provides the details. He has yet to recover from a serious infection contracted a few weeks back. He has yet to recover from the resultant hospitalization. His blood pressure is out of control, as is his blood sugar, as is his five-time-daily kidney dialysis. There is more, but what I register most deeply is that my father cannot stand or walk unaided, will not eat. He wants to spend his days in bed, face to the wall, so to speak, and he does.

Then there is this: my son will be handed over to me today at exit B of the underground subway station near his home in Shau Kei Wan, as if he were a parcel, a newspaper, or a forgotten lunch box that needed to be passed from one person to another quickly and efficiently. The meeting is scheduled for one-thirty in the afternoon. His "auntie" will wait with him near the turnstile, watching for my approach along the tiled corridor. She — three years his foster mother — will hand me bags full of clothing and toys, kiss him good-bye, and walk away, heart bleeding. We will wait until she is out of sight, then together retrace my steps back to the train that will take him away from the only safe home he has ever known.

Neither my father nor my son at their respective stages of life should have so much asked of them. My father's life reads like a dictionary definition of bravery — he has fought wars, saved lives, risked his own, stuck it out when others gave up. Now he is eighty-four and tired. His life will never again be easy; if he is to live, he will have to rise each day ready to fight. My son was three years old when he was yanked, bruised, bleeding, and malnourished, out of an abusive home. Now he is being yanked away again, this time from a family who loves him, but cannot offer him permanence. No matter that the yanking is being done for his own good: he is six, and he must start over.

So where will the courage come from? None of us can say.

It has been suggested to me that I might find something beautiful, something transcendent, about the juxtaposition of this moment — life ending, life beginning. This should not be much of a stretch for me. I often fall for the sentiment, even at its sappiest, when it is played out in movies or books. I go for it in the abstract, that is. But now, facing down the trade-off, things are looking ugly. It's a pretty raw deal for the person on the short end of the life stick, no? How could I have missed that? Call it the circle of life, call it transitions, call it God's plan, or nature's way: from where I stand at the moment, it makes poor work of grief and confusion and fear. I welcome my son. I am terrified of losing my father. I detest the idea that the coming is linked to the going.

Is this bitterness or selfishness that I am tasting? The question will have to wait; the day is forcing itself on me. In lieu of courage, I will act on routine. Be pragmatic, follow the steps. Break each task into its smallest component parts and swallow the parts whole, one after another, without thinking. I have done this in worse times, and I know it works. I will shower and dress. I will make coffee and check the ferry schedule. I will call my father. I will meet my son. I will let the momentum of the day carry me through, and hope for so much more than that for my sick father and frightened son.

Home

A FISHING BOAT woke me early this morning just as dawn was crossing the water. The sound of its outboard motor dissolved my dream, but it was an odd sound — a repeated kerplunk, kerplunk, kerplunk — that fully roused me. I looked out my bedroom window to see a sampan with a crew of three, their faces obscured by battered, wide-brimmed straw hats, moving slowly past my line of sight about fifty feet from shore. One of the crew was sitting in the stern with a hand on the tiller, guiding the boat on a course parallel to the coastline. Another was casting out a net. The third was standing at the bow, rhythmically hitting at the water with what looked like an industrial-sized toilet plunger. The noise, I guessed, must serve to bring the fish to the surface and drive them into the net. I watched from my bed until the boat passed out of sight. Eight miles to the east, Hong Kong Island was just becoming visible, it's skyscrapers back-lit by the rising sun. A pair of noisy, red-whiskered bulbuls, one of the most common birds in southern China, hopped among the small stretch of brush that separates our bedroom window from the South China Sea, their black crests and red vents flashing like secret signals amid the vegetation.

It was time to get the day started. We had moved over the weekend, and our apartment was crowded with boxes that needed to be unpacked and sorted. It's a task I usually dread, but this time, I was looking forward to establishing my claim to this new place. I was home.

Moves, for me, have little to do with geography and everything to do with identity. "I define who I am by defining where I speak from," writes Canadian philosopher Charles Taylor, deftly capturing in one sentence a truth I've spent years chasing. Taylor's meaning may seem self-evident to a life-long New Yorker, or a rancher, or an Israeli. It should have been obvious to me, for I was once deeply influenced by place. But I lost the thread in pre-adolescence and have only recently picked it up again.

Now, finally, with some serious schlepping around under my belt, I have come to understand that no matter how fine a city or town I find myself in, my degree of comfort with the place is determined not so much by what it has to offer, but by an instinctive sense of "fit." Does the place where I stand nurture my sense of self? This is the criteria I have come to apply against the concept of home.

My identity — my definition, in Taylor's apt words — begins in the Deep South. Mine was a lazy, dreamy childhood, the best and happiest parts of which unfurled outside in the dirt and grass. The pine trees and the grand weeping willows, the crickets, garden snakes and dandelions, even the paved streets softening in the Louisiana sun like a stick of butter: these were my playmates, languid, inviting, ever-fascinating.

I might devote a summer's afternoon to the black-tarred road, rippled and sticky in the midday heat, fascinated by how the melted surface tugged at the soles of my rubber sandals. I could as easily spend hours squatting in the dirt poking at anthills, delighted when I could trick the ants into marching up and over my hand or foot. I loved the exaggerations of nature that flourished in our sub-tropical climate: the thicket of blackberry bushes that had overtaken the empty lot across the street, the tangle of wild honeysuckle that grew along the border of our backyard, the waxy-white gardenias blooming by our front door with their impossibly heady scent — this is the stuff of my childhood. I was steeped in the flavors of the South, never knowing nor caring where the boundary lay between me and my physical environment.

That ended abruptly when I was ten and we moved to Seattle. It was a wrenching experience. The Pacific Northwest, though beautiful by even the most exacting standards, felt alien and inhospitable to me. Part of it was a lack of light: because of its far-northern latitude, Seattle has a dark, drawn-out winter. And part of it was the mist and rain that seem to go on endlessly. The sky, shrouded for months on end in leaden gray clouds, closed in on me. The earth was no longer welcoming. I had lost my place in the world, and with it, the remains of my childhood.

The girl I was in Louisiana bore little relationship to the adolescent I became in Seattle. Grief and bewilderment hardened into anger; the anger fed depression. It was impossible to explain the changes to my concerned parents since I did not fully understand them myself. I missed what had nurtured me: the intensity of the light and heat, the wildness of the landscape, the profusion of colors and scents but, at ten, I was unable to fit words to the feelings. I had felt porous in Louisiana, as if I could exchange essential bits of myself with the natural world. In Seattle, I lived defensively and held myself tight against the damp, the rain, and the darkness.

As an adult, I tried Alaska, Italy, Palo Alto, and San Diego. I bumped around in New York for a bit. I returned to Seattle and a few years later gave it up again. North Carolina came close, but my husband wasn't wild about it.

Hong Kong was a lark, an adventure. We were meant to be here for two years. Bill would work across the border in Guangdong Province running a manufacturing plant. I would finish what I had begun in North Carolina: a master's degree and a television documentary project. I would have time to devote to my writing and to my children.

We took in Hong Kong like enthusiastic tourists. We toured the bird market, the flower market, the night markets, the jade market, and the wet markets. We explored the botanical gardens and sampled Chinese opera. We visited Buddhist temples, lit incense coils, and watched as tiny birds selected bits of paper to tell our fortune. We went on hikes through the hills and explored the coastal fishing villages. We tried food we could not identify and learned how to use chopsticks. We took weekend trips to Hanoi, Phuket, Beijing, and Shanghai.

Hong Kong is a crowded city, with a population of seven and a half million people (roughly equivalent to the population of Switzerland) jammed into just over one thousand square kilometers, and because of that life often spills out into the streets. Much of the display is ordinary: laundry, cooking, grandparents playing with their grandbabies, raised voices, pets on the loose.

But a good deal of it is intimate. Bill and I once sat at our favorite (and crowded) open-air bar and watched a woman in an apartment across the alley making her bed and changing her shirt without a hint of discomfort. One of our favorite hiking trails takes us through a small village, Nim Shue Wan, where the houses, made out of cement blocks and corrugated metal, more often than not have their doors thrown open. For a quarter of a mile or so, taking two steps off the trail would land us in the middle of someone's living room.

The openness drew me out. At first, I chalked it up to curiosity. I would often walk through the city for hours, watching and listening, absorbed in the scenes I witnessed. But I soon realized that something else, or something more, was going on: I was finding my place again, marking my territory, as it were. Despite the apparent foreignness of Hong Kong, I had discovered that the city fits me in the same way that Louisiana fit. It is familiar to my senses. I know the light. I grew up with the heat. I know what baked streets smell like. Even the South China Sea lapping at the rocks outside my window is familiar in its immediacy, in the way that it lures me back into the physical world.

One of the fishermen picks up a strip of cloth from the bottom of the sampan and wipes his face. I wonder if he can see me as clearly as I see him. He glances up and briefly raises his arm. Is he offering a greeting, or shooing away a fly? I mimic his motion, just in case. Hong Kong is a place where life offers an open invitation, and I have accepted.

Superman made real

"Aiiiyaaa!" my son shouts as he flings his arms towards the ceiling, dashes across the living room, and leaps over our cat, Lucy, who until that moment had been resting quietly on a stack of floor cushions. Wai Ming tosses his red cape back over his shoulders and readies himself to reverse course. "Mommy, see me!" he shouts, meaning, *watch me*. Lucy tolerates one more leap, then removes herself to the top reaches of our television cabinet. No problem. Wai Ming adds another cushion to the pile to take her place, backs up and vaults. "See me!" has, in the excitement of it all, become garbled, and I listen to a rapid-fire litany of "Shimmy! Shimmy! Shimmy!" until a botched landing quiets him down.

Like a legion of other little boys, Wai Ming has spent the week prior to Halloween strutting around the neighborhood in his new Superman costume, practicing Superman tricks, and trying out Superman's action vocabulary. *Pow! Take that! Oof!* Kryptonite makes no sense to him, Lois Lane is beside the point, and the Clark Kent charade is a mystery (why hide out as a mild-mannered newspaper reporter when you could spend all your time as Superman?), but the rest — the super-human strength, the bad guys, the fights, the flying — has crossed all language and culture barriers and is firmly implanted in the imagination of one impressionable six-year-old Chinese boy.

The costume, which my husband brought back from the United States, has earned us big points with Wai Ming, and trick-or-treating, once he figures out how it works, should significantly up the score. This is only the second time that we have done something as a family that is so entirely new to Wai Ming that he cannot find a similar experience to draw on. His reference, his rock, his source of everything good, is Mrs. Loi, his former foster mother. "Loi Tai," he'll say enthusiastically if we have cooked a familiar meal, or visited a familiar Hong Kong landmark, or even bought him new clothes, new toys. "Loi Tai," he says approvingly, indicating that the experience in question is known to him and that he can locate the object or event somewhere on the internal map of okay things that he carries in his mind.

There is, though, a prick of discomfort for me in this all-around happy Halloween feeling, and that is the plastic mask that comes with the costume. It is standard issue, featuring wavy black hair, extra-thick black eyebrows, a square jaw, white skin that looks as if it were molded from melted-down ping-pong balls, and round holes for eyes. It might be that any number of parents are momentarily unnerved by the exchange of child for comic-book character, but with Wai Ming, the oddness shades into grotesque. It is not only the impossibly bad racial surgery that the mask imposes on my son, his skin stripped of color, his handsome Asian eyes rounded out in a look of blank, stupid surprise, his slender face muscled up — there's more to it than that, though that in itself makes me shudder.

The real problem is that the transformation effected by the mask hits too close to home, mirroring the job that the adults in his life have seemingly given him. The instructions are not explicit, but he must feel them, nevertheless, hanging over his head every waking moment. *Here's your new family; here's your new life. Make it fit.* How can he know that this responsibility is not his, that an inside-out makeover is emphatically not what we want from him or for him? I worry that, from his perspective, the delicate process of folding into our family feels like a full-frontal attack on his identity. I worry more that he might be right.

All adoptive parents can tell you where they were when they got the call. I was at the beach. It was a glorious day in late April, and I had accompanied Sera and Natalie's kindergarten classes on an outing to Repulse Bay. Unlike Hong Kong's northern shore, which undergoes constant face-lifts in the form of virtually non-stop land reclamation projects, as well as demolition, construction, and reconstruction of its buildings and infrastructure, the south side's rocky coastline is relatively untouched. The north shore, with its face turned to China, is chock-a-block full of high-powered, let's-make-a-deal energy. The south side is its slower, more relaxed tropical cousin featuring exquisite, largely unobstructed views of the South China Sea punctuated by sandy beaches, sampans trailing fishing lines, and clusters of rock-strewn islands. Much of the coastline backs up to the soft greens and browns of mountain terrain. Its distance from the island's financial center in the Central district has checked development to some extent; nevertheless, the natural beauty of the area is a lure for many of Hong Kong's wealthy residents, and a number of the exclusive neighborhoods and luxury apartment buildings on the south side command some of the highest real-estate prices in the world. The beaches in the sheltered bays along the coast are one of the selling points, and on warm summer days they are packed to capacity.

Since the fieldtrip was held on a weekday in spring, we had ample room to spread out, even though we were a big group — roughly one hundred and fifty kids from eight different preschool classes, as well as parents, teachers, and nannies. We had just finished climbing off the chartered buses and I was digging around in my beach bag for sun block and insect repellent when Anna called.

Preoccupied by the kids splitting off in different directions and the pandemonium endemic to such an event, I momentarily missed the significance of the call. I hadn't phoned Anna in months and expected nothing but bad news from her. When she told me that Wai Ming's biological mother had relented and signed off on the paperwork freeing him for adoption, I was dumbstruck. "Oh boy, oh boy," I repeated, while my command of the English language took a short holiday.

I paced the length of the beach with my mobile phone pressed to my ear and tried to corral my concentration. "What happened?" I asked. "I thought his case was going to court." Anna had few details — all she knew for certain was that the social worker assigned to his case never let up and eventually, she won. "Do you think. . . ?" I began. Anna did not need to hear the rest of the question. "No guarantees," she responded. Wai Ming was free for adoption, and his case would go before the matching panel in two weeks. We would have to wait it out, not knowing if other families were interested in the child I again began to consider my own, or whether the panel members would consider us an appropriate placement for someone with his background. Anna was rooting for us, and I had to leave it there. I spent the rest of the picnic studying every pre-school aged boy I came into contact with, trying to imagine what my own family might look like in a short time.

The only feeling that broke through the suspense of the next two weeks with any clarity was fear. This, I had not expected. Rather, I expected it at some later date, the exact timing of which remained comfortably vague in my mind. But instead of floating around in a bubble of happiness, or, more realistically, biting my nails in nervous anticipation, the full sweep of the commitment we had made hit me like a rock, and doubts crawled out of every crevice.

It may have been a reaction to the surety — extreme, I recognize in retrospect — with which I had tackled the adoption process, my husband, Anna and, through her, the Department of Social Services. I never dared admit to having second thoughts; I was afraid it would be fatal to the process. I went at it with all of the stubbornness of a donkey and the delicacy of a bull. This is hardly uncommon among adoptive parents: we fight hard, then harder, to clear the hurdles between our children and us. We lower our heads and transform ourselves into battering rams. We're ready to take on any comers — government bureaucrats, social workers, doubtful family members — none of them stand a chance. Ask around; you'll not believe the lengths your neighbor went to hold her adopted baby in her arms. Such is the power the children we have yet to meet wield over our lives.

But pretending to be infallible does not make one infallible, and the collapse of that particular pretense was ugly. What's more, my timing was terrible. Now that there was a real life dangling at the end of my ambition, my ability to hold fast was more important than ever. But instead of digging in for the final push, I panicked and looked around for someone else to hold the rope.

Bill took over. I equivocated; he held steady. I gave voice to every misgiving that wormed its way into my consciousness. He heard me out, and more, responded honestly. I confessed to wanting to back out of the deal. Time to close ranks, as my father is fond of saying. Our family of four suddenly seemed the perfect, manageable size. A known quantity. What if I *had* misjudged the impact an adoption would have on Sera and Natalie? What if I discovered I couldn't love a virtual stranger?

"What if you were right in the first place?" I asked Bill in one of my meltdown moments.

"We'll deal with it," Bill replied. "Together, as a family." And he meant it. Having never felt the need to pretend to one hundred percent certainty, he had coped with his own doubts with far less *sturm und drang* than I was experiencing. Thus it was that Bill was ready and facing forward when we got word that Wai Ming had been matched with us, while I was still flat on the ground, anxiously trying to find my feet.

Imagine what it must have felt like for Wai Ming.

If love has a face, it surely belongs to Loi Tai, Wai Ming's extraordinary foster-mother. With the exception of three weeks spent in emergency care, Wai Ming had lived with Loi Tai ("tai" means wife, hence *Loi Tai* translates as *Loi wife*), her husband, Loi San (*Loi husband*) and their two teenage daughters Rachel and Phoebe, since he was taken from his biological family. The family in general, and Loi Tai in particular, took in a badly hurt little boy and swaddled him in love. They loved him as if he were their own. They loved him through difficult periods of acting out. They loved him, and loved him more, until his wounds began to heal under the bright light of their care. They were obligated to feed him, clothe him, take him to the doctor, the dentist, to school. They were obligated to provide him with a few toys, to take him on an occasional outing, to treat him with kindness and respect. They did so much more. To say that they are good people, to say that we will forever be grateful to them, only brushes the surface.

Our first precious picture, a three by five snapshot, is given to us by Loi Tai. Wai Ming, wearing a school sports uniform, is posed outside under what looks to be an open-air walkway. Palm trees are visible in the background. He is smiling, and looks happy and relaxed. Is he missing his top two front teeth? I can't make it out. I have copies made and send the photo to Wai Ming's soon-to-be grandparents, aunts and uncles, friends. I show it around to anyone who will look, including strangers. We frame the original, and put it up next to Sera and Natalie's baby pictures.

We have another picture, this one cut from a Chinese daily newspaper and given to us by Anna. Wai Ming is three years old and adorable. His hair is shaved close to his head, accenting the handsome symmetry of his face and, again, he is smiling cheerfully. The rest of the photo and the accompanying text tell a different story. Wai Ming is sitting on a hard, molded plastic seat at a crowded McDonald's restaurant in Kowloon. Next to him are two policemen in their warm-weather green uniforms. They are waiting for his mother to show up; she had deserted him there for the second time in as many months.

The newspaper reports that he entertained himself as best he could for more than two hours, wandering from table to table and in and out of the restaurant, until worried staff called for help. He did not cry, nor act distressed. The police finally escort Wai Ming home to his grandmother. No one knows where his mother has gone. The police report, along with the newspaper clipping, are added to his file at the Department of Social Services. It gets thicker, but not yet thick enough to remove him from his home.

That did not happen until he had been abandoned for the third time. His mother had lost custody of Wai Ming to his grandmother, but that did not stop her from taking him from their family apartment while his grandmother was at work. Three days later, he was found in a daze, roaming the halls of his grandparents' building, trying to find his way home. He was bleeding from ugly wounds on his forehead and arm, hungry, dehydrated, and badly frightened. Parental rights were terminated, and his mother was sent to prison for her role in the abuse.

Wai Ming spent the next few weeks in a hospital ward, recovering. Despite what he had been through, he has happy memories of his time there. He had ample food, other children to play with, toys, and lots of attention from the doctors, nurses, and social workers. He had fun — perhaps for the first time in his life.

Our first meeting was arranged. Bill and I would wait for Wai Ming outside of his kindergarten class. Loi Tai and Anna would wait with us and introduce us when school let out for the day. If all went well, we would walk Wai Ming home. (I wanted to ask Anna what could possibly go wrong in the two minutes, tops, it would take to complete the introductions, but reasoned that now was a good time to be as compliant as possible.)

I could not decide what to wear. This does not happen to me often, since I rarely change out of shorts and a tee-shirt during Hong Kong's warm weather, or jeans and a tee-shirt during cooler weather, but if there was ever a time to fancy up a bit, this was it. Or was it? Should I dress to appeal to a little boy, in which case, my usual would suit, or did I still need to impress Anna with more grown-up clothes, in which case, maybe a skirt would be more appropriate?

Bill refrained from rolling his eyes at my clothes confusion, since he was having the same problem. We settled on shorts and casual shirts, agreeing that there was no point in carrying the responsible-parents charade too far, but made sure that they were spotlessly clean and pressed. Without meaning to, we both ended up in tan shorts, white shirts, and brown sandals. We eyed each other in exasperation, but, having spent too much time dithering around in front of our wardrobes, changing was out of the question. We rushed out of the house feeling like the Bobbsey twins gone wrong.

The long trip, first by ferry, then by subway, to Shau Kei Wan on the far west side of Hong Kong Island, gave us plenty of time to get wildly nervous. This was one whopper of a blind date we had gotten ourselves into. At least we were well chaperoned. Waiting along with us for the school bell to ring were Anna, Loi Tai and her daughters, and enough bystanders to fill a casting call for a crowd of extras. No one was shy about this; the kindergarten is located in the courtyard of an enormous public-housing complex, and the area near its entrance filled up quickly with old men and women shuffling curiously towards Bill and me.

My guess is that we were the only Caucasians within a mile or two. I probably could have ducked my head and escaped notice since my five-foot frame is average in Asia, but Bill, at six-foot-three, stuck out of our gathering like a misplaced telephone pole and literally turned heads as he walked by. Some of the more interested spectators walked right up and joined our little group, smiling and nodding at each of us. A scattering of others dropped their grocery bags and stood staring from a distance, occasionally calling out comments to friends across the way. The discordant notes of Chinese opera floated from a portable radio left unattended on a cement bench. Two ancient men dressed in pajamas studied a chessboard. The smell of French fries and hamburger grease drifted toward us from the McDonald's in the complex's shopping arcade. Anna was making small talk with Loi Tai. Bill was trying out his Mandarin. I was dying a slow death. I couldn't decide if I wanted to storm the kindergarten and get it over with, or run for cover.

Long after I thought I could not bear to wait another moment, the doors opened. A blur of children — blue and white uniforms, black hair, frenzied energy — whizzed past us. Predictably, a clump of kids skidded to a stop, doubled back, and surrounded us. Bill and I stood grinning like idiots (neither of us wanted to be caught without a smile on our face), trying to sort through the crowd and spot our future son. Finally, after what was surely an eternity, Loi Tai shot off toward the open doors. Wai Ming, looking as wary as a cat surrounded by a pack of overly-friendly dogs, was being escorted out by a cluster of women (the school principal, her assistant, and two of Wai Ming's teachers, I later learned). Wai Ming was moving slowly, Loi Tai quickly, and she had time to take him by the shoulders and whisper instructions in his ear before giving him a small shove in our direction. He stuck out his hand, and did his best to say "Nice to meet you" in English, then ducked behind his foster-mom. I envied him that; I would have liked to hide behind Bill.

With the introductions completed, we broke away from the crowd and set off toward the Lois' apartment in one of the nearby towers. Public housing in Hong Kong is a different creature than its counterpart in the States. With some notable exceptions, it functions as it was designed to, providing safe, clean, relatively inexpensive housing for lower- and middle-class families. The Lois, along with thousands of other Hong Kong residents, had bought their apartment under a government financing plan intended to boost home ownership. They will most likely stay there for the rest of their lives. It is a nice bit of security for Wai Ming.

We had expected to say goodbye at the door, but Anna's arrangements for the afternoon were superseded by Loi Tai's spontaneous invitation to "Come in, come in!" We were all glad to follow her lead. She ushered us in, hustled us in, really, and darted into the kitchen to make a pot of Chinese tea. Wai Ming disappeared into his bedroom. If he was curious about us, he hid it well. I didn't mind — it gave me a bit of time to relax my face, collect my wits, and look around.

Their apartment, I noted with relief, looked much like our own, only on a smaller scale. A tidy six hundred square feet was divided into three small bedrooms, a combined living and dining room, two bathrooms and a kitchen. It was also furnished much like ours, with the exception of a corner of the dining room that was devoted to an ancestor shrine. The similarities between our apartments would, I hoped, shave off one small corner of Wai Ming's upcoming culture shock.

Loi Tai returned with hot tea and two photo albums. Together, with Anna as translator, we delved into the last three years of Wai Ming's life history. I was struck by how completely he had integrated into the Lois' household. There were pictures of Wai Ming at a family wedding, pictures of him visiting amusement parks and museums with Phoebe and Rachel, pictures of him celebrating Chinese New Year, his birthday, and Christmas, surrounded by his foster family and their relatives. Where we had expected to find evidence of vulnerability, we found security; where we had expected anger, hurt, or at the very least, uncertainty, we found happiness. It was strikingly clear that he was not just another foster child passing through on his way to a "real" family. Taking him away was going to be excruciating. Some bonds would only be loosened, but others would be destroyed. Was it possible that we all — Bill and I, Anna, the Lois — had made a huge mistake in agreeing to this adoption?

We would later have a long, worried talk with Anna about the Lois. Wai Ming was the second foster child they had taken into their home. They knew from the beginning, Anna reported, that he would eventually be placed with a permanent family. For reasons that remain confidential (although I guessed financial, rather than emotional, in nature), the Lois did not — could not, most likely — apply to become Wai Ming's adoptive parents. The child who had arrived in their home prior to him had already moved on to a new family. Wai Ming, then, was familiar with the process of placement, and knew that it would eventually be his turn. Loi Tai had done her best to prepare him, but it was visibly painful for them both. The best we could do was to ask the Lois if they would be willing to stay in his life, to be a part of our extended family, to provide Wai Ming with an extra link to his Chinese heritage and culture, and, not least of all, to help strengthen his psychological armor. They agreed almost before the words were out of our mouths, and have since stuck to their promise.

The next few months of our lives lurched forward with a strained awkwardness that wore us out. We made numerous trips to the Lois' home to visit Wai Ming. We took him on brief outings and watched him cautiously circle around us, keeping a defensive distance. We were as friendly as we knew how to be, smiled as much as we could, and made clumsy attempts to engage him in chitchat. Communication, though, was one-way and stilted, since every word had to pass through a translator. Wai Ming, who, we have since discovered, is at heart a chatterbox despite those first few months of silence, directed his attention and energy towards those around him who spoke Cantonese and quickly made friends with Anna and the bilingual young woman who had volunteered to act as our escort. I trailed along behind them feeling like a third wheel. Did this child know what I was to be to him?

While the question was rhetorical at first, I soon began to ask it of Anna in earnest. Had anyone told him that Bill and I were going to be his parents? He had to know what was going on — or did he? The answer, we discovered, was muddied, and for good reason. The Department of Social Welfare tries to give older children a say in their placement. If a child is dead set against a particular match, and remains adamant for some indefinite period of time, the match might not move forward. This makes the social workers cautious about prematurely labeling prospective parents "mom and dad."

Wai Ming's case, though, was slightly different. It's not that he did not like Bill and me. The problem was that he did not want to leave the Lois and did not understand why, if they could keep him for three years, they couldn't keep him forever. It was not a question Bill or I could answer, so we stood aside and let Anna and Loi Tai handle the explaining and negotiating. From what we could gather, they approached the subject obliquely and allowed Wai Ming ample room to maneuver. Translated, it meant that for an unspecified period of time he would know us primarily as the nice American family who hung around a lot and occasionally brought him toys.

It also meant that we had to cool our heels during a two- or three-month getting-to-know-you period as dictated by the Department of Social Services. I visited Wai Ming once a week while Sera and Natalie were at school and Bill was at work. On weekends, we'd all go. (I asked for permission to visit him more often during the week, but that proved too disruptive for the Lois.) And while we did not make much headway in our personal relationship with Wai Ming during those months, we did learn a great deal about him.

Each visit started with the adults sharing a pot of tea and trading information across the kitchen table. Loi Tai, being extremely protective of Wai Ming, dug as far as she dared into our personal lives. I answered her questions as honestly as I could. I owed her that. In turn, I quizzed her about the contents of Wai Ming's heart. Is he loving? Angry? Defiant? Shy? Moody, aggressive, needy? What scars does he carry from his time with his biological mother and her boyfriends? Does he like to be touched, or does it frighten him? What's he like with other kids? At school? I needed information, it is true, but what I was really after was reassurance. I wanted to hear Loi Tai say, *He's a good kid, you'll love him,* which she did with such conviction that I came to trust her assessment of the adoption more than my own.

Some information, important information, came our way almost accidentally. One afternoon, Anna joined me for my mid-week visit. It was a hot, sticky day and Loi Tai pulled the apartment windows shut and flipped on the air conditioner before serving us tea from a thermos. Wai Ming was in his room playing with a stack of Legos. The heat had claimed our energy, and the conversation drifted loosely as we blew into our cups. I mentioned to Anna that I was still curious about the matching process.

"Did we have any competition?" I asked, expecting to be told that it was not information she was allowed to share.

"Yes," she said, "from a Chinese couple."

"Really?" I sat up in my chair. "How'd we win out?" I asked crassly.

"Well," she answered, "they were concerned about his speech impediment." It must have gone well beyond "concern." The caseworker representing the couple had a professional obligation to try to place Wai Ming with a Chinese family. She would have worked hard to convince them that his speech impediment was minor and responsive to therapy.

"So what happened at the panel meeting?" I asked, leaning in closer. "Did you have to argue for us? Did anyone object?"

Anna took a moment to mentally convert the conversation from its original Cantonese into English. "I told my colleagues that Bill had a similar problem as a boy and had enrolled in speech therapy." She stopped for confirmation, and I remembered that during our home study Bill had told her in passing that he had once spoken with a lisp. We weren't even talking about adoption at the time. We were talking about Anna's mastery of English, and Bill's repeated attempts to correctly pronounce some of the more difficult sounds in Mandarin. He told her it was much harder than ridding himself of a lisp. And there it was. When he was six, Bill had a course of speech therapy to correct a lisp. It was proof positive that we would not hold the problem against Wai Ming. That's what tipped the decision in our favor — a random remark that could have just as easily never been uttered.

I have a friend who has adopted two infants from China. She was told that the bureaucrats in China were careful to match the child's personality to that of the adoptive parents. Margaret, however, suspects that they take the top file from the stack at the left of their desk, the top file from the stack at their right and staple them together. There you have it. Parent and child are matched. Our experience was not random, not by a long shot; still, I am awed by the hit-and-miss element of adoption that is impossible to eliminate. Luck swung our way on this one, and I count my blessings.

Wai Ming moved in with us on August 5th, distressed, sad, and frightened. Natalie and Sera immediately got down to work trying to make him comfortable. (To my great relief, they were thrilled with their big brother and lorded it over their friends who were unlucky enough to get stuck with a newborn.) To mark the occasion, Natalie volunteered to share her favorite blanket. Sera, certain that the best our family had to offer was our cat, tried repeatedly to force Lucy to sit in Wai Ming's lap. Some of their efforts were rehearsed — I was counting on them to help ease the transition for Wai Ming, and we had talked about the things they could do to assist him in sorting out his new environment. In the end, though, I think their rambunctious eagerness overwhelmed him. He spent most of that first day sitting quietly on the sofa fiddling with an electronic hand-held game that had been given to him as a gift.

Bill and I did not fare much better in our efforts than did Sera and Natalie. We coaxed Wai Ming gently, we coaxed him playfully, and although he was unfailingly well behaved and did his best to respond to our overtures, his heart was clearly elsewhere. He coped, it seemed, by trying to become inconspicuous. He watched Sera and Natalie carefully and mimicked their behavior when possible. He was meticulous about following our house rules. He could easily spend half a day without saying a word. It was a pattern that altered very little over the next few months. Beyond putting on a run of Disney movies, which seemed to fully engage his attention, we had no idea how to pass the time. I had never witnessed a six-year-old child (and certainly never a six-year-old boy) exercise such ruthless self-restraint. It was like living with an agonizingly polite houseguest.

We floundered. Our communication was painfully limited. The easiest of jobs was an ordeal. We endured elaborate games of pantomime just to get breakfast on the table. I had numerous friends who spoke fluent Cantonese lined up to translate for us, but I could never convince Wai Ming to speak to them on the phone or in person. We relied heavily on Anna, who checked in on us frequently, to pass hunks of information back and forth like an overburdened carrier pigeon.

Still, I often had to lead Wai Ming around like a blind man. A close inspection of his mouth showed a collection of black stubs. I took him on the first of many visits to the dentist without being able to adequately explain where we were going and why. Same for the trip to the doctor's office for a round of vaccinations. He was stoic about major outings like these, but would cry over small, seemingly inconsequential misunderstandings, such as not being able to ask me if we were taking a taxi or a bus back home. On occasion, it would come to a head, vastly overwhelming his ability to cope, and he would curl up on the sofa and sob, while we stood by, badly shook by our inability to make it — make *anything* — better.

It was not supposed to be like this. According to my personal fantasy of what it meant to be a good adoptive mother, I was supposed to be offering this frightened, vulnerable child unconditional love, oodles of support, and tender kindness. I was supposed to be the good fairy. Instead, I was often exasperated and snappish by the end of the day. My patience was thin. I was tired. I wasn't living up to my expectations, and I was wallowing in guilt because of it. I felt as if I had been cast in a role that I thought I knew well, only to discover that I had not learned my lines and was on stage with an indifferent leading man. *Have we done the right thing?* The question shadowed my days, and I probed my heart for love with the same compulsiveness that a child brings to wiggling free a loose tooth. Please God, I prayed at night, let me learn to love this boy.

Routine helped, granting us moments of ease that were sometimes big enough for both of us to step into. I could lay out his school uniform and know that he understood what would happen next. He could hold up his soccer ball and a questioning face and I knew that he wanted to play outside with the two boys who lived next door. He caught the rhythm of our evenings: dinner, followed by baths, pajamas and cleaning teeth, followed by quiet play, followed by books. He attended to each step like a pro.

We learned how to hold conversations — a few words sprinkled among lots of gestures to create sentences, even paragraphs, about topics that became familiar through repetition: the fruit display at the grocery store (he loved picking out the ripe mangos), the mobile library truck that arrives in our neighborhood every Tuesday, the puzzles and building blocks that he eventually started taking down from the shelves. We both learned to string out our patience past all reasonable expectations in hopes of reaping a small reward. Wai Ming still crows about his inventiveness in taking me by the hand, leading me to the refrigerator, and pulling out a container of orange juice in order to demonstrate which pajamas he wanted to wear to bed. "Oh," I said, "you want the pajamas with the little orange balls on them." "Yes!" he shouted in delight. That night we both went to bed happy.

One afternoon in the late fall, Wai Ming's kindergarten teacher, who is also a close family friend, phoned. She told me that during a quiet moment at school when she had been helping Wai Ming with a phonics worksheet, he had, without preamble, looked up at her and announced that he no longer wanted to return to the Lois' house. He had decided to stay where he was.

The call turned my heart inside out. At six years old, Wai Ming had found the courage to make an irrevocable decision with such far-reaching, life-altering consequences that it would disarm many an adult. And he did it knowing that nothing would ever be the same for him from that moment on — not his family, his language, his nationality, or his culture. Understanding who he is, absorbing all of the disparate elements, may well be a life-long process for him. Still, he chose us, just as we had earlier chosen him.

The flame was lit. Maybe it had been all along, but I was so caught up in searching for a particular, familiar kind of love that I missed it. I was anxious to be a good mother to Wai Ming, and the only template I knew how to work with grew out of my relationships with my daughters. What is growing between Wai Ming and me is messier, tougher, more deliberate, and more frightening. It did not spring up instantaneously and fully formed, as did my love for Sera and Natalie. This new relationship needs a slow cooker.

I love my son. I admire my son.

Superman has never looked so good.

Magic potions

SERA DISAPPEARED into the bathroom yesterday after asking me in an overly polite voice for a small plastic bottle. "Please," she added quickly. She invited Natalie and a playmate to step in, invited me to step out, then closed and locked the door. "I'm making a magic potion," she announced through the door. "Okay," I hollered back, "but you three must promise me that you won't drink it." "We promise," they chorused.

One might wonder, at this point, about my parenting skills — or, more likely, about my common sense — and I must admit it took a good deal of self-control not to peek through the keyhole. But I had my reasons for leaving them unsupervised. It had been weeks since Sera had said "please" to me on her own volition. It had also been weeks since she had initiated an imaginative game. She has been going through what parenting books call a stage of disequilibrium. Briefly put, she was having a growth spurt — physiologically, or cognitively, or emotionally, or perhaps all three — and it was too much for her to take in. She had lost her equilibrium. Translated, that means she was shouting a lot, and demanding a lot, and clinging a lot, and crying a lot, and basically driving me mad, mad, mad.

The books recommend patience and understanding, as well as a firm hand and well-defined boundaries. I agree wholeheartedly with this advice. Following it, though, is a different story. Patience and understanding withered under the onslaught of Sera's temper. A firm hand and well-defined boundaries took some nasty hits as well as I scrambled to regain control of my household. "How long will this last?" I wailed to my friends. "When will I get my real child back, the loving, kind, fun child that I adore?"

Now, with my ear cupped to the door (cheating, I know), I heard my daughter laughing. She was cooperating and sharing. She had invented this game without any help from me and did not need me to be glued to her side to carry it out. Did I dare hope that she had reached a turning point? I took a gamble, stepped back, and held my breath while my daughter mixed her magic potion.

A half-hour later, the three girls emerged. The potion was done, and Sera was anxious to share the recipe. Mix together shampoo, glitter, baby oil, white flower oil, bath soap, and milk and voilà, you have — well, you have a mess, that's what you have. And, in my case, one very happy child.

My father's story

THE NORTH KOREAN SOLDIERS captured me at a roadblock near Taejon, South Korea on the evening of July 20, 1950. At the time, I was a Lieutenant in the U.S. Army and weighed 165 pounds. I was marched two miles back to Taejon and placed in the upper floor of a brick building along with approximately 130 other American prisoners of war. I was stripped of all personal belongings, including wristwatch, ring, wallet, dog tags and shoes (I was shoeless until we were turned over from the North Koreans to the Chinese in October 1951). We were not fed for the first thirty-six hours, nor permitted to have any water. When we were fed we were given about 250 grams of cooked rice per day. To the best of my knowledge, wounded prisoners were not given any medical attention.

We left Taejon on foot for Chochiwon on July 23, 1950, marching about thirty-five miles and arriving on July 25, 1950. No medical aid was administered to the wounded during this march. We received about 200 grams of cooked rice and very little water. At Chochiwon, we were confined in the upper story of a wooden building and fed about 300 grams of cooked rice twice daily. We were denied water and latrine privileges for an entire day. Prisoners were not permitted to stand or lie down during the day, but had to sit at attention. Wounds were not treated, and one man died of a stomach wound.

We left Chochiwon by rail on July 29, 1950, and arrived at Chonan, a distance of about 25 miles, that same day. We did not receive any food or medical treatment during this movement. At Chonan we joined another group of American prisoners bringing the total to approximately 200 prisoners of war. We were forced to sit at attention during the day, with no room to sit at night.

We left Chonan for Seoul on or about July 30, 1950 by rail with about 200 prisoners. Wounded personnel were inadequately treated en route. North Korean soldiers, who frequently mistreated prisoners by either cuffing or kicking them, guarded us. No deaths resulted during this movement.

We arrived in Seoul on or about August 5, 1950, where we joined another group of American prisoners, bringing the total to 350 enlisted men and officers. We left on or about August 10 by rail for Pyongyang. Here we joined another group of American prisoners, bringing the total to approximately 726 enlisted men and officers. Although some attempt was made to treat wounds, seven men died here for lack of proper medical care. Captain Boysen, captured medical officer, said that the limited medical supplies and medical knowledge of the Koreans would not help the wounded prisoners.

We left Pyongyang, traveling by rail, on or about September 5, 1950 with 719 POWs in the group. Two enlisted men died for lack of medical treatment. One man died of dysentery. The other had a leg wound which became infected, and he bled to death. We arrived in Manpojin on or about September 11, 1950 with 717 prisoners and were housed in an old Japanese camp on the outskirts of Manpojin overlooking the Yalu River. We remained there until October 10, 1950. We received some medical care, but eighteen or nineteen prisoners had died here from lack of adequate medical care and malnutrition. We left Manpojin on foot for Kosan, about fifteen-mile distance, arriving the same day. We arrived with 698 prisoners, inadequately clothed for the winter weather. Sixteen blankets were issued for the 698 prisoners. Approximately thirty percent of the POWs had received some item of winter clothing, which was found in an old warehouse and was inadequate for cold weather. To the best of my knowledge, thirteen prisoners died here from malnutrition and lack of medical care. Two others were shot by civilian police while attempting to escape.

On October 19, 1950, we left Kosan on foot for Dyakan, approximately thirteen miles southwest, arriving the same day. We now had about 685 prisoners and were fed one meal per day of soybeans for five days. The camp commander and officers had left the camp and were not seen again. Both food and medical supplies had run out and none of the Koreans attempted to purchase or otherwise acquire food for the prisoners. Korean civilians furnished two or three of our meals. Approximately eight prisoners died in this camp from malnutrition, beriberi and pneumonia.

We left Dyakan on foot on October 24, 1950 and returned to Kosan, arriving the same day. During this march, a Korean guard pulled one enlisted man out of the column and left him on the side of the road. The enlisted man had dysentery and could not keep up with the column. We left Kosan the following day and returned to an open field about three miles west of Manpojin, marching about fifteen miles and arriving the same day. We left five or six enlisted men behind at a police station in Kosan; these men were weak from malnutrition and could not march. We were informed several days later by a Korean officer that the Korean police executed these men. No shelter was provided for us between the 25th and 29th of October, 1950. We lived on field corn and Chinese cabbage soup when available. No medical facilities were available, and about thirteen prisoners died from exposure and malnutrition.

On October 31, 1950, we were released from Army control to the control of the civilian North Korean police. We were ordered to march to Chunggan, which lies approximately eighty-three miles northeast of Manpojin, using the main road alongside the Yalu River. By the order of the camp commanded (nicknamed by the prisoners as "the Tiger") we left sixteen American prisoners behind. These men, we were informed by the guards several days later, were executed. In the following eight days, sixty-five prisoners died on the march, sixty of them shot to death, the other five dying from exposure and malnutrition. Two civilian women were shot to death because they could not maintain the pace with the column. One was a blind French nun and the other a Russian woman who had been interned by the Koreans. Mistreatment of prisoners was frequent. Prisoners were kicked, cuffed, and beaten with sticks and rifles without reason. Prisoners did not received medical care of any kind, were not clothed properly, and about seventy percent did not have shoes and were forced to march barefooted through the snow and freezing weather. The bulk of the prisoners did not receive any shelter on three or four of the night halts. Food was inadequate; we received approximately 250 grams of millet, and a like quantity of semi-cooked cracked field corn on alternate days. Prisoners were not permitted to use latrines at night, causing men with dysentery to soil both clothing and surrounding sleeping areas. For this, the guards normally beat them. We arrived in Chunggan with about 571 American prisoners of war guarded by about sixty to seventy-five police guards on November 8, 1950.

We left here on November 11, 1950 for Chunggan-ni, about six miles east, arriving the same day. We were housed in a school building and Korean homes. Prisoners were placed in rooms in such numbers that it was impossible to sleep at night. We were fed twice daily, cornballs and soup. We were permitted approximately forty pounds of wood per room to burn in stoves in sub-zero weather. No adequate medical or sanitary facilities were available. Prisoners were frequently beaten and punished by guards. A lieutenant in the 24th Division was beaten by a North Korean officer, resulting in his death two weeks later. We lost about 150 men in this camp during our stay, all deaths resulting from malnutrition, starvation, dysentery, beriberi, exposure, and pneumonia. We were guarded by North Korean civilian police.

We left Chunggan-ni in April 1951 and marched six miles west to Chunggan, remaining in this camp until October, 1951. We lived in crowded, filthy conditions without adequate bathing facilities. About 140 prisoners died here from malnutrition and lack of medical care. We knew this camp as Camp #7.

On or about October 15, 1951, we left Chunggan and marched eastward following the road along the Yalu River for approximately forty miles. We were then loaded on river barges and poled downstream for two days. On the third day a power launch took us in tow and we arrived at our destination in Chongson on October 19, 1951. We received meager meals during this travel, consisting of rice balls and soup. We had no medical treatment nor any shelter while on route. By this time my weight was down to as low as 80 pounds.

From November 1951 to August 1953, I was confined in Camp #2, Pingchon-ni, under the control of the Chinese Communist Forces. Although I witnessed no beatings or torture in this camp, two men who tried to escape were confined in a doorless shack in sub-zero weather without heating facilities for sixteen days. In general, treatment was fair, except for so called "study periods" (brainwashing) and mental strain forced on us by the Chinese. We remained at this camp until August 18, 1953, when we started our trip for repatriation.

The procedure in Kaesong, where we were finally housed before release, was that each evening all POWs were paraded and the Chinese read out a list of names of those who were to be released the following day. We knew then that September 6th was the last day for release, so as the first week in September progressed nearer the sixth day, the number of POWs decreased each morning. Each evening the tension rose as the names were called out. The ever-dwindling number of those left began to wonder if their time would come: the possibility of the Chinese retaining hostages after the sixth had not escaped our minds, particularly in my case because the Chinese had threatened that I would never be released. This was a result of a heated discussion we had the night before regarding the merits of capitalism versus communism.

After the release on the 5th, those remaining knew they had twenty-four hours to go — or else. The Chinese kept well out of sight the whole day as if to purposely increase our anxiety. As evening drew near, we waited for the whistle to blow for roll call and to hear our names called for tomorrow's release. True to form, there was no whistle at dusk and there was no roll call. No one slept; we lay and sweated and worried.

I remember sitting on a rock waiting for my name to be called. Because the Chinese did not like me, I was told again that I was not going to be released. Finally, when they called my name, I told them no, I was not leaving. Of course, this disturbed my captors and they insisted I must leave.

On the morning of September 6, 1953 we were given our morning food and then paraded and bussed in a Chinese army truck. At last we were on our way. We were at a Y-road junction and saw a large Chinese army truck approaching. When the truck reached us, we saw on board hundreds of South Korean POWs who were also being released. We proceeded south to Panmunjom where we were released at last. For whatever reason, I was one of the last American POWs to be released. By this time I had regained some of my weight and I weighed 140 pounds.

I remained in the service until 1963 and retired as a Lt. Colonel.
Charles Minietta
Seattle, Washington
Spring, 1989

The snow silenced the soldiers' footsteps. With solemn faces and clipped, military precision, they squared off on the powdery-white grass, two rows of three each. A gust of cold air caught us as we sat mutely inside the hall witnessing the ceremony through the open glass doors. We heard their hands slapping metal as they raised their rifles, heard the firing mechanisms lock into place. Three shots rang out, counted silently by each of us, fired in unison by the members of the Fort Lewis Honor Guard. They had come to bury my father.

I laid my head on my husband's shoulder and wept.

The temperature dropped precipitously on the last day of my father's life. We woke to a thin coating of ice that clung like a glaze to the world outside our windows. My stepmother, Mary, and I had been following the weather reports with trepidation. Snow, unusual in Seattle, even at the end of December, carried with it troubling questions. What if an ambulance couldn't get through? What if the power went out and we couldn't keep my father warm? What if the delivery of his kidney dialysis supplies was held up? We discussed contingency plans over our early-morning coffee, then took our breakfast to the back bedroom to eat in my father's company. He no longer had any interest in food, but made the effort to sit up and take a bite of toast for our sakes. Mary and I made small talk, took care of his medical needs, then left him to rest.

The house was unusually quiet. Sera, Natalie, and Wai Ming, who had flown out with Bill for the Christmas holidays, were playing outside, enchanted by the ice-world so unlike anything they had seen in Hong Kong. Bill and my sister, both of whom had to return to work, had reluctantly left Seattle the previous day. My brother, who lives nearby and had been stopping in most days, had not yet arrived. We put away a few more of the Christmas decorations and then tiptoed down the hall to check on my father. The bedside lamp was switched off, but the strings of small, white Christmas lights that we had used to make the room festive threw off a soft glow. He was awake, lying quietly with his head turned toward the sliding glass door that opens out onto the back deck. "Look at them," he said, smiling, and pointing outside. The kids, freed from adult supervision, had turned the ice-slicked wooden planks into an impromptu skating rink and were twirling, sliding, and crashing with abandon. Peals of laughter punctuated their play. "Are they warm enough?" my father asked, still watching through the window.

We knew why he was asking. He had spent much of his time in the last few weeks with his thoughts focused on the frozen countryside of North Korea, reliving a seminal experience in his life.

The captured soldier was shoved into a small, bare room in an abandoned school house. The North Korean in charge of the interrogation looked him over, then snapped, "Who is your commanding officer?" The soldier remained silent. "Answer!" the officer demanded, but again, received no response. One of the guards motioned for the soldier to move about ten paces toward the wall, then raised his 45-caliber pistol and leveled it at the soldier's head. At the last moment, the interrogator reached out and slapped the gun away.

My father, Charles Minietta, was a prisoner of what has aptly been called "the forgotten war." It began on June 25, 1950, when the North Korean People's Army crossed the 38th parallel into South Korea. Within days, thousands of South Korean troops had been captured or killed, and on June 28, the capital city of Seoul was taken. The United States, fearing a total collapse of the south, led United Nations troops in defense of South Korea. It was the beginning of the Korean War — a nightmarish conflict that lasted thirty-seven months and cost hundreds of thousands of lives.

My father was a thirty-three year old army captain, stationed in Japan and assigned to the 24th Infantry Division occupation troops, when the war broke out. The division, like the rest of the U.S. military, had been drained by the demands of World War II and was ill-prepared to fight another war. Nevertheless, they were the closest to the battlefront and the first to be shipped out.

The troops landed south of Seoul in early July. They were short of weapons, short of ammunition, and what equipment they did have often did not work. Many of the soldiers were new recruits, having been called up and packed off as quickly as possible. There had been no time for basic training, and a shocking number of them had not even learned how to fire their rifles. My father tells of one soldier under his command who reported for duty wearing tennis shoes; no one, apparently, had taken the time to issue him combat boots.

Within twenty-four hours of landing, the few hundred men that formed the advance detachment of the 24th Infantry Division found themselves facing five thousand well-armed and well-trained North Korean troops. It was a stunning, brutal experience, as North Korea smashed through the American lines with ease. The Americans fell back in an attempt to defend Taejon, the temporary capital of South Korea, but were spectacularly unsuccessful and suffered heavy casualties. Taejon fell to the North Koreans, and the American forces were once again forced to retreat. The 24th Division had lost more than 3,500 troops in just over two weeks.

It had been my father's job to oversee the evacuation of the American military personnel and heavy artillery from Taejon. After sending off the last trainload, he looked around, as he put it, and realized that his commanding officer, along with the rest of his unit, had already shipped out, leaving him behind with no transportation. He was captured a few days later, and spent the remainder of the war, thirty-six months in all, as a prisoner. His survival was nothing short of a miracle. During the first eighteen months, when the captured U.N. troops were held by the North Koreans, 500 out of 700 prisoners died.

A handful of men paced away the long night, stopping frequently to shake awake those who slept. "Come on, get up!" they urged. "You've got to keep moving!" "Get up, god damn it." The temperature was well below zero; sleeping on the frozen ground for more than an hour or two at a time, particularly in their weakened condition, could cost them their lives. The men stomped their feet and slapped their arms against their bodies in a constant, losing battle against frostbite. As the morning sun rose, the guards poked the butts of their rifles into the cluster of prisoners huddled together for warmth. Most were able to rise to their feet, but a few more frozen bodies were added to the death toll.

During the late summer and the fall of 1950, the North Korean army guards kept their prisoners on the move, marching them north in an effort to evade advancing enemy troops. The men were in shockingly bad condition. After months of existing on a starvation diet, disease, namely dysentery, beriberi, and diarrhea, had taken a heavy toll. Untreated battle wounds and infections plagued many of the prisoners. Others suffered serious injuries from beatings. A captured American missionary, Larry Zellers, caught a glimpse of the prisoners at a rail station in early September, and later wrote in his autobiography, *In Enemy Hands,* "I couldn't believe what I was seeing. These ragged, dirty, hollow-eyed men did not look like any American soldiers that I had ever seen. I had worn that same uniform until five years before, but I could hardly recognize it on the men walking along that railway platform in front of me. The North Koreans had provided no special consideration for the wounded. Some of the more badly injured prisoners were half-carried by companions; others limped along as best they could. Communist guards walked alongside and behind the POWs but made no attempt to assist in any way. We were all so stunned that we watched in silence."

As bad as it was, it soon became worse. By late October, the North Korean forces were in disarray. They had suffered a significant setback in mid-September when the Americans landed two divisions well behind enemy lines at the port of Inchon, and again at the end of the month, when American troops retook Seoul. The North Korean lines broke, and their forces fled north. U.N. troops gave chase, determined to push as far as the Manchurian border. The most immediate consequence of this turn of events for the prisoners was a desperate lack of food and medicine. But far more significant was the arrival of a new camp commander who took over when the military handed off control of the prisoners to a civilian police guard.

The new commander — "the Tiger" — announced that the exhausted, starved prisoners would begin yet another march — this one, deep into the snow-covered mountains of North Korea to Chunggan. The men protested. They knew many of them would die

if they undertook another forced march. The commander's answer
was blunt: "Then you will march until you die." They covered the
distance in eight days. Sixty-five prisoners died along the way.

The Tiger assembled the prisoners on a small hillside. "Who's respon-
sible?" he barked. During the day's forced march, a number of men,
ill, wounded, starved nearly to death, fell out of line, and were left by
the side of the road, unable to take another step. The North Korean
guard, the Tiger, was furious. He ordered the ranking officers from
among the prisoners to line up in front of him. "Which of you lost the
most men?" he demanded. Lieutenant Cordus H. Thorton stepped
forward. The Tiger turned him around, shoved his hat forward over
his eyes, and shot him in the back of the head.

The execution had its intended effect. The prisoners understood
that their lives were on the line at every moment. They could just
as easily be beaten, shot, or left for dead by the side of the road as
not — all at the whim of one man. The basic rules of humanity
had been upended, and the death march set the stage for the rest
of their captivity under the command of the Tiger.

The surviving prisoners spent the remainder of the winter in
barbaric prisoner-of-war camps, where hundreds more lost their
lives. Adding to the horror of their experience were the extreme
weather conditions. In 1950–51, North Korea was hit by record-
breaking cold, with temperatures falling to a low of forty below
zero. Many of the prisoners were clothed in nothing more than
the remains of the summer-issue uniforms that they had been
wearing at the time of their capture. The majority wore rags for
shoes. The prisoners were forced to spend a number of days and
nights with no shelter. The shelter they did have was dilapidated,
dangerously over-crowded, filthy, and cold — bitterly, relentlessly
cold. The guards took full advantage of the weather to punish
their captives, who were sometimes singled out at random. It was
common, for example, for the guards to strip a man from the waist
up, douse him with a bucket of water, and force him to stand
outside in the snow until he collapsed. Pneumonia claimed many
lives.

Years ago, when I initially started talking to my father about his time in the camps, he reduced his experiences to a few short stories. *"We were given two balls of rice a day. Maybe some watery soup."* Or, *"We lived like animals. We were filthy, never allowed to bathe, and covered with lice."* He'd give a quick shake of his head and change the topic of conversation. It wasn't until I started attending ex-POW reunions with my father that I heard a different kind of story.

"Did your dad tell you about the cigarettes?"

"What cigarettes?" I asked.

"Well, some of the guys were so addicted to tobacco that they would trade their rice ball away for a cigarette, or at least, what passed for a cigarette in camp. So your dad, whenever he was sent out on wood detail, he'd steal a few tobacco leaves from the fields, and then roll 'em up. He'd wait for the guys coming out of the food line, and offer them the tobacco. But first, he'd stand there and make them eat their rice ball. Saved a few lives."

Another of his buddies told me that my dad nearly died on the death march.

"Yes," I acknowledged, nodding.

"No, I mean because he kept trying to carry the men who couldn't walk any farther," he said. "Your dad knew they'd be shot. So he kept trying to carry them, even when the guards beat him for slowing down the column."

But the story that was told most often was the one about the blanket:

Sixteen blankets, 700 men, bitter cold. Night falls, and the prisoners collapse, exhausted, in the open field that is to be their shelter for the night. One, their ranking officer, is close to death; probably won't make it through the night. A lieutenant notices, unfolds his blanket, silently tucks it around the freezing man. They both live through the night, through the march, through the war.

Shortly after my father's death, my friend and pastor, Marybeth, showed me a passage written by Martin Luther King, Jr. It read: "If a man happens to be thirty-six years old, as I happen to be, and some great truth stands before the door of his life, some great opportunity to stand up for that which is right and that which is just, and he refuses to stand up because he wants to live a little longer and he is afraid his home will get bombed, or he is afraid that he will lose his job, or he is afraid that he will get shot, . . . he may go on and live until he's eighty, and the cessation of breathing in his life is merely the belated announcement of an earlier death of the spirit.

"We die when we refuse to stand up for that which is right. We die when we refuse to take a stand for that which is true. So we are going to stand up right here . . . letting the world know that we are determined to be free."

Two very different men, two very different lives; and yet, they share this: as young men, they found their beliefs, their morals, their very lives tested in ways they could not have foreseen. And in those moments, they did what they believed to be right, no matter the cost. I wish they could have met. What a conversation that would have been.

The flight back to Hong Kong was lonely. I had been in Seattle for a month, burrowing as far as possible into my father's world. Part of what I was after was a degree of physical intimacy that my father had not previously allowed. We — Mary, my sister and brother, and me — helped him to the bathroom, fed him his meals, cleaned his feet, combed his hair, helped him shave. We sat with him during his dialysis, took his daily blood sample, recorded his blood pressure, and measured his temperature. We were trying to coax his body into sticking it out, even though he was clearly ready to let go. He tolerated our efforts without a single complaint — literally — knowing that we were desperate to pour out a healing love, but his attention had turned inward.

Again, we were allowed in. It was a rare privilege. My father rarely spoke of his war experiences when I was growing up. I didn't know that he had been held captive until I was in my early teens, and even then, when the information slipped out at the dinner table, he was unwilling to go into detail. Like many of his compatriots, he believed he could walk away from the camps and leave the trauma behind him. When he was in his sixties, he started, tentatively at first, to attend ex-POW reunions. The more he got drawn in by what they had to offer, and by what he had to offer in return, the more I got drawn in. Here, at last, was a chance to mine some emotional information about my father — something he was not good at communicating until late in his life. So I heard the stories, and I discovered why so many of his buddies considered him a hero.

Not that he would accept the tribute. "I did what I was trained to do," he'd tell me. "I was a soldier, and good soldiers take care of each other." That was his line, and he stuck to it until the last few weeks of his life. A succession of visitors, ex-POWs whose friendships meant a great deal to my father, came to sit at his bedside and trade stories. What passed between them was raw and honest. "I love your dad," they'd say on the way out, and I knew that they had said it to him as well.

A Christmas card was the last blow to his emotional barrier. The card was from Colonel Dunn, the man with whom my father had shared his blanket. Colonel Dunn had written to say goodbye to my father, and his message was heart-breaking. It read in part: *This is the saddest time of my life, including the time we spent in POW camps together. You have been the best friend I have ever known. You have done more for me than any other including my own family. Chuck, I have thousands of times thought of the bitterly cold night on the death march when you generously shared your blanket with me. I doubt I could have survived that night without your help. You are by far my greatest friend.* When I read him the card, he cried. Later that afternoon, when we were sitting together sharing the silence, he said to me, "Colonel Dunn told me that I was the bravest man he ever knew." It was the first, and last, time I had ever heard my father acknowledge his own courage.

Shortly after the funeral, my mother, who had remained on friendly terms with my father and step-mother, mentioned that she was puzzled by how my father's prisoner of war experiences had become the dominant theme of his — and our — lives during the previous months. He had lived most of his twenty-three years with my mother acting as if it had never happened. The facts and details: those we could coax out of him. But questions about how he felt — those seemed to genuinely puzzle him. "What does it matter how I felt?" he once answered me. Anger, he would admit to; anything that the anger might have covered up — fear, desperation, hopelessness — stayed under wraps. Now, the experiences that were once stripped dry seemed to have become the current that carried all the pent-up emotion of a life-time. When he looked back over the years, the time he spent in camp was clearly the epicenter. As for me: "I went where he went," I told my mother. It was the only option on offer if I wanted to understand his life on the same terms that he understood it — and I did. I urgently, passionately did.

My children, wrapped in airline blankets and slumped every which way in their seats, have finally fallen asleep. They are anxious to get home to their father, their friends, their school. It will take a few days for the worst of the jet-lag to pass, and then they will step back into their routine without missing a beat.

I sit listening to the quiet sounds around me, unable to relax into sleep, and wonder how to move forward in this world without my father. An odd thought breaks through the grief: his death has shoved me into adulthood. But how could that be? His death did not take me by surprise. He was eighty-six, and his health had been failing for some time. And, of course, I've been an adult for decades, and, for the most part, have assumed the concomitant responsibilities with gladness and competence. But not in this way, not without the rock of my father to lean against. I feel as if I have been handed a hot baton in the middle of a race. My first instinct, my heart's desire at this moment, is to drop it.

No. I will take my father's baton. It is courage and honor and selflessness. It is well-made, solid, and trustworthy. I will take it down a different road, and, eventually, hand it on to my own children.

We touch down at Hong Kong International Airport at Chek Lap Kok. I turn to the East, and ready myself for the next chapter in my life.

Acknowledgements

I am particularly grateful to Melissa Malouf, Assistant Professor of English at Duke University for her encouragement and magnificent editing skills. I also owe much to the wonderful community of students, professors, and administrators involved in the Master of Arts in Liberal Studies program at Duke University.

To all of the amazing women (and girls) particularly close to my heart — Fran, Mary, Lynn, Leslie, Paula, Marybeth, Sera and Natalie — I owe a world of thanks. I love you all. Karmel, thank you for your many insights and words of encouragement. Wai Ming, my dear son, you have inspired much of this book. Your courage shines bright before me. Bill, you're the best. Thank you for everything.

About the author

Robin Minietta, a journalist by training, worked for over a decade as a reporter and producer for public television in the United States. She has numerous awards for her broadcast work, including an Emmy. Her essays have been published in literary and academic journals in the U.S. Minietta lives in Hong Kong with her husband and three children.

CPSIA information can be obtained
at www.ICGtesting.com
Printed in the USA
FSHW02n0633210918
52443FS